COMPUTATIONAL APPROACHES
to
TEXT UNDERSTANDING

A Survey of Current Issues
in Denmark

edited by

Steen Jansen
Jørgen Olsen
Henrik Prebensen
Torben Thrane

Institute of Informatics
Faculty of Letters

Museum Tusculanum Press
UNIVERSITY OF COPENHAGEN

© Museum Tusculanum Press & the authors, Copenhagen 1992
Printed in Denmark by B. Stougaard Jensen
Cover design: Thora Fisker
Computer typeset by Institute of Informatics, laser printed
ISBN 87-7289-181-5

This book has been published with the financial support of:

The Publication Committee at the Faculty for the Humanities, University of Copenhagen
The Danish Research Council for the Humanities
Department of Computational Linguistics, Copenhagen Business School
Faculty for the Humanities, University of Odense
Framework Programme in Cognitive Science/Aalborg University
Institute of Informatics at the Faculty for the Humanities, University of Copenhagen

Museum Tusculanum Press
Njalsgade 94
DK-2300 Copenhagen S

CONTENTS

Presentation   5

Aalborg University
Per Hasle and Peter Øhrstrøm: *Counterfactuals and Branching Time in Automated Text Understanding*   13
Inger Lytje: *Cognitive Grammar and Text Understanding*   29

University of Odense
Poul Søren Kjærsgaard and Lene Schøsler: *A Valency Based Description of Danish Verbs*   45

University of Roskilde
Ole Ravnholt: *Cognitive Models as Discourse Representation*   61

Center for Language Technology
Susanne Nøhr Pedersen: *Frozen Expressions in Danish and French*   75
Bjarne Ørsnes: *Negation in Eurotra: An Attempt at Determining the Scope of Negation for NPs*   89

Copenhagen Business School
Michael Herslund and Finn Sørensen: *Verb Valency and Automatic Text Processing*   105
Lita Lundquist: *Indefinite NPs in Legal Texts. An Application of Electronic Dictionaries in a Textlinguistic Study*   115
Bodil Nistrup Madsen: *Lexicon and Terminology*   129

University of Copenhagen
Jørgen Olsen and Steen Jansen: *Which Rules Can Be Used in Automatic Text Analysis?*   141
Henrik Prebensen: *A Formal Approach to Dynamic Text Interpretation*   157
Torben Thrane: *Dynamic Text Comprehension*   173

Presentation

Steen Jansen

This volume contains the written versions of the papers presented at a seminar (November 1991) on computational analysis of Danish texts, organized by the Institute of Informatics, Faculty of Letters, University of Copenhagen, and supported by the Danish Research Council for the Humanities.

The aim of the seminar, which brought together researchers and students from different Danish milieus of computer science working with text understanding[1], was to provide a forum for an informative and benificial exchange of positions adopted, models developed, experiences made and problems faced by people working in the field. It was equally our hope that the seminar would give a broad picture of the actual research and work in progress in Denmark.

In the invitation to participate at the seminar, the focus was set on *texts* written in *Danish*; however, since this was so far the first seminar specifically centered upon this subject, these terms were given a quite comprehensive meaning: texts are necessarily written in natural language, so problems related to natural language processing will equally be problems of text understanding, and experiences with other languages will be of general interest and *eo ipso* of interest for Danish. Consequently we did not present a precise list of specific problems (or questions) to be faced by the speakers at the seminar.

As it happens, the seminar presented a wide range of different approaches to the problem of text comprehension, and of interests in distinct aspects of the text in itself. In spite of these differences, the reader will notice an effort to face all the problems under one common device, that of text analysis.

It is evident that text analysis, computational and otherwise, is far less advanced than analysis at the sentence level and below - if by analysis one means a procedure based on arguments and concepts which can be intersubjectively identified, and resulting in proposals, which can be discussed in detail and partly used by others without having to accept (or reject) all or nothing.

In a not so distant past, text analysis has been approached from two rather unrelated angles: from a literary criticism point of view to which the text has often been the more or less contingent expression of a message which could meaningfully be seized only when confronted with a complex world outside the text; and from a linguistic point of view where the basic problem was to

---

[1] Not all Danish researchers in this domain could participate in the seminar, and, unfortunately, having other obligations some of the speakers at the seminar have not been able to present their contributions for this volume.

explain, in operational terms, the difference between a sequence of disconnected sentences and a sequence of connected sentences making a text. Often the insight - in the 'essence' of the text - seemed more appropriate in the first than in the second approach, despite the lack of precision and operationality.

Today, with the emergence of computational analysis, this difference has been transformed into an opposition between a cognitive view, holistic or top down, and a linguistic approach, more analytic and bottom up; the first starts from the high level notion of understanding in general: a text, a whole work or even human behaviour as such; the second begins with the single, concrete elements of the text and tries to follow a path up to greater and greater groups of elements forming units. There has sometimes been very lively confrontations, one approach denying the value or usefulness of the other. Future advances in text analysis, however, surely rely on successful cooperation and mutual comprehension between these seemingly opposite points of view. As Leech formulates it (about a sligthly different opposition)

> the two approaches are complementary: they are, we suggest, digging the same tunnel from opposite ends, and at some future time may meet somewhere in the middle. (...) In so far as these complementary research programmes are successful, they will tend to eliminate the differences between the results of the two types of methodology. In fact, the two methodologies will probably contribute to one another's success. (Garside, Leech and Sampson: *The computational analysis of English*, 1987, 4)

On the one hand, it seems to me that the seminar, presenting rather different points of view, opened some new ways to the problems of text analysis: it may be noticed for example that the former key notion of *coherence* only appears in five out of twelve contributions (Ørsnes (only once), Lytje, Ravnholt, Prebensen, Olsen and Jansen) and in the last two of them in a sense considerably different from the traditional one or as a rather problematic device; on the other hand, the seminar showed that common problems can be identified beyond fundamental methodological and theoretical divergences.

In order to outline some areas of fundamental importance, I will use the traditional distinctions, however general and necessarily rather simplified they are: on the one hand, a distinction between a *more linguistic* (or computational linguistic) approach and a *more cognitive* (or cognitive science) approach (without giving a very strict definition of the two terms), and on the other, a distinction between four 'levels' in texts: *words*, syntactic *constituents* (syntagmes/phrases), *sentences* (propositions/clauses) and *text*.

Based on these distinctions, the papers of the present volume could be ordered in the following schematic way (which does not presume to give a more detailed reading of every paper; evidently more than one paper covers more than one single domain).

SURVEY

← COGNITION   *   LINGUISTICS →

WORD-LEVEL

Inger Lytje
(parsing with semantic frames)

Bodil Nistrup Madsen
(specific terminology)

Poul Kjærsgaard and Lene Schøsler
(valency and lexicon)

CONSTITUENT-LEVEL

Bjarne Ørsnes
(negation scope and reference)

Lita Lundquist
(indefinit NP and reference)

Susanne Nøhr Pedersen
(idiomatic expressions)

Michael Herslund and Finn Sørensen
(valency and ...

SENTENCE-LEVEL

... situation semantics)

TEXT-LEVEL

Torben Thrane
(understanding and referential function)

Ole Ravnholt
(cognitive models and text structure)

Jørgen Olsen and Steen Jansen
(inference and unification)

Per Hasle and Peter Øhrstrøm
(temporal logic and counterfactuals)

Henrik Prebensen
(formal logic and interpretation)

There are two contributions on the topic of vocabulary or lexicon seen from a linguistic point of view: they deal with a specific vocabulary and a single word class.

Bodil Nistrup Madsen deals with the problems of how to organize the lexicon of technical terms in the legal vocabulary, in order to treat correctly questions for information to a legal knowledge base (in this case about corporations). The specific actual problem is to identify terms for the different concepts in the area and the relations between these concepts, using the text under consideration, i.e. the *Danish Companies Act*. But often such terms and concepts are not given exact definitions in the law, so the necessary information cannot be extracted from this text alone.

Poul Kjærsgaard and Lene Schøsler propose a description of Danish verbs based upon valency structure; one purpose is to construct databases either for uses in language teaching or to establish a more direct link from lexicon to parsing. The actual work is centered around the search for well-founded tests, based on negation and pronominalization; they are applied to some examples of verbs in manifested sentences, with a view to identifying the correct valency schemes corresponding to possible readings of the sentences. Their examples document the lack of consistency in the entries in traditional dictionairies, and the strong need for explicit rules. A lexicon editor has been implemented in Hypercard.

Inger Lytje approaches the problems of word sense and grammar from a cognitive point of view and wants to establish a narrow link between semantic parsing and text comprehension. Parsing is a bottom up process which is not rule governed but considered a sequence of interactions between linguistic entities. There is no proper grammar in the traditional sense, nor an independent world knowledge database; all knowledge is stored in a frame based lexicon organized as a semantic network which can be extended, reorganized etc. according to new knowledge; it contains, for example, the fundamental valency relations which characterize the linguistic entity. The theories proposed by Langacker provide many of the fundamentals, especially the assymmetric *trajector-landmark* relation, used by Inger Lytje. A prototype lexicon for Danish words has been implemented, and so has the first step in the parsing process where all words in a given text are tagged with the relevant lexical information. The second step where syntactic and textual structures are built up from this information is in the project phase.

Four contributions have been assigned to the domain of syntactic constituents; the last one, by Michael Herslund and Finn Sørensen, deals with verbals, but also with the entire sentence, thus forming a transition to the next section.

The contributions by Bjarne Ørsnes and Lita Lundquist both deal, at least partly, with problems of reference, the first in relation to the scope of negation, the second in relation to indefinite noun phrases.

Bjarne Ørsnes proposes methods for calculating whether a noun phrase is inside or outside the scope of a negation, determined on syntactic and semantic grounds. This question depends on the relative position of the negation and the noun phrase (as the quantifier scope in standard logic), and on referential and morphosyntactic characteristics of the noun phrase combined with contextual determination. General strategies for the calculation, adopted in translations between European languages, are formulated, and their application to Danish is discussed. Precise rules of calculation are necessary for correct translations, and so, evidently, to establish a correct basis for the interpretation of a text. The entire issue naturally implies pointers to the domain of sentences.

Lita Lundquist uses a set of tools, specifically developed for French, i.e. different electronic dictionaries and user programs allowing the user to construct local grammars for the search of specific constructions or constituents in running text; the principles however can be used on Danish texts as well. The grammars set up by Lita Lundquist find all the tokens of indefinite noun phrases and, despite the restrictions imposed by the available tools, make it possible to draw conclusions on empirical grounds about the distribution of indefinite NPs in different types of legal texts and their relations to discourse referents. She suggests that further studies of these aspects should go in a semantic-textual direction.

The problems dealt with by **Susanne Nøhr Pedersen** concern a certain group of idiomatic expressions, generally formed as sentences with the verb *være* (to be), looking for a possible general structural description of them, instead of listing them wholesale in a dictionary. Distinguishing six types of such expressions, Susanne Nøhr shows that the determining element is not the verb, but the first, and obligatory, prepositional phrase of the expression; and she proposes, especially in connection with interfaces for translation purposes, that such expressions should be given a specific representation, different from the normal, more valency oriented one, where the central PP should be placed, as the governing element, at a "higher level" than the verb. Obviously such proposals, by which dictionary search would be replaced by analysis of text segments, are of interest to text processing.

The last contribution placed in this section, by **Michael Herslund and Finn Sørensen,** deals partly with the syntactic properties of the valency schemas of verbs, partly with the sentence as a provider of information about a situation. Understanding is defined as a relation between an agent, a text, its information and (relevant) situations. The first part mainly treats the problem of discriminating bound valency terms (complements) from free terms (adjuncts), especially when both are prepositional phrases, in order to identify the arguments of the verb and the correct relations between them, and thus the entities and the situation referred to. The second part (which is the only one I have placed in the section on sentences) is on *Situation Semantics* and introduces the notion of *infon*; this serves, together with the valency scheme, to secure the relation between the verb and the formal representation of the situation, which the sentence is about, and thus serves as a tool in the search for information contained in the text, explicitly or implicitly.

Although all the contributions, in my opinion, point to at least some sort of textual problems, I have assigned five contributions to a distinct section on texts. Their principal purpose is not to study single text elements at sentence level or below, but rather to propose or to discuss models of the overall representation of the text or the process of text understanding/comprehension.

Torben Thrane adopts a cognitive point of view, within which text comprehension is defined as a special case of NL understanding. In a broad review of the field up to now, he argues that too much attention has been paid to making descriptions of texts more and more detailed, and too little to making it clear what the goal of text understanding processing should be. For him understanding is a matter of dynamic information processing which establishes, enlarges or changes memory structures, named computable representations. Comprehension becomes manifest only in responses to questions about the text. On these grounds Torben Thrane proposes a theory of categories, especially of nouns and of referential functives, and ways of dealing with them as information carrying quantities.

Ole Ravnholt discusses Johnson-Laird's mental models and proposes to replace them by cognitive schemas. These should be combined with grammatical structures in the construction of representations of the content of the text. Such representations not only use, but also include world knowledge and knowledge about the linguistic forms of the text. The text is divided into discourse segments by linguistic structure, and the whole text as well as each segment has an intentional (or planning) and an attentional (or focusing) structure; the content of each segment is modelled by a focus space, and these focus spaces are placed on different stacks according to the current state of the discourse. It is shown how search for resolving purposes and anaphors works inside this stack structure.

Outside the domain of cognitive science and psychology, **Jørgen Olsen and Steen Jansen** place their contribution in a philological, or textlinguistic, tradition and present on these grounds an elementary model of inference. The succesful result of an inference (i.e. an answer to a question about the text or the information in it) is a conclusion drawn from premises; these can be found in the text, or it can be necessary to start a search for additional premises outside the text. Since the implementation tool is Prolog, i.e. declarative programming, the automatic inference mechanism ultimately relies on the unification process, but the alternative 'inside *vs* outside' leads to a distinction between an immediate, or simple *unification*, and a mediated unification, or *inference*. It is suggested that Toulmin's argument schema could be a useful tool to guide the search for supplementary premises.

Per Hasle and Peter Øhrstrøm present the notion of branching time as a formalism suited for an analysis moving from sentence level to text level, here exemplified in a specific case: a text constructed on counterfactuals. In contrast to a classical approach, this formalism allows them to take into account a basic property, the dynamical dependency of counterfactual implication on information in context. From an actual state (or world) in the textual course of events, different possible states (or worlds or histories) can be outlined, one of which will be the realized future; the statements of the text can be evaluated and related to each other. An application of the branching time formalism is demonstrated using a specific program (CIMP); it allows them to construct a time ordered tree representing the text structure and offers a formalized representation of each statement on which precise rules of evaluation can be applied.

The contribution by **Henrik Prebensen** proposes a formal approach to text understanding, based on the practice of literary text analysis and historical text critical methods on the one side, and on standard concepts from systems of logical deduction on the other. Text understanding is here considered a theory and a practice clearly distinct from the ones formulated for similar projects in Cognitive Science. Information extracted by logical deduction in accordance with a strategy organizes into a reading. Understanding a text is thought of as an activity in which a human agent, a reader, asks a question, which expresses some puzzling problem. He then tries to find out if there is information - in the text alone or in the text plus other accessible texts expounding text-independent assumptions accepted by the reader - from which an answer can be logically deduced. If there is no or only partial information, there can be no answer - neither for the machine nor for a human agent.

Counterfactuals and Branching Time in Automated Text Understanding

Per Hasle and Peter Øhrstrøm
Aalborg University

0. Introduction
The aim of this paper is two-fold. For one thing, we wish to discuss certain properties of counterfactuals which call for an evaluation procedure that is sensitive to information in the surrounding text. We shall indeed describe such a procedure, although not in all details. The other issue with which we are concerned is the notion of branching time (BT). Branching time is related to the former topic, since a semantics for counterfactuals can be stated in a natural manner in terms of a BT-model. We shall suggest that the notion of branching time is of general importance within Automated text understanding. We may then see the evaluation procedure for counterfactuals as just one concrete example of how some of the properties of a dynamical textual environment may be described in terms of BT.

1. Semantics of Counterfactuals
The general form of counterfactual statements can be exemplified by the sentence

    (S1)   If the electricity hadn't failed, (then) we would have had dinner on time.

We may view S1 as the result of applying a formation rule R to two sentences S2 and S3:

    (S2)   The electricity didn't fail.
    (S3)   We had dinner on time.

That is, R(S2,S3) = S1. From a syntactical point of view, it is an intricate task to spell out R in detail, since the formation of counterfactual statements from two sentences has a number of repercussions on negation and tense within those sentences. We shall leave this issue aside, since it is not of primary concern to this paper.

  Obviously, counterfactual statements are a sort of conditionals, but they differ from ordinary material implication in a number of respects. The very linguistic form of S1 strongly suggests that the antecedent is known or expected to be false. The general problem then is how to evaluate the truth value of such sentences, and to determine how they may enter into Natural Language Understanding and, more specifically, Automated text understanding. For the sake of completeness it should be noted that the antecedent need not be false, although that is usually the case. If the antecedent happens to be true, the *counterfactual implication* (CI) simply coincides with material implication. The following inference is accepted as valid:

1. If the electricity hadn't failed, (then) we would have had dinner on time.
2. The electricity didn't fail.
---
3. We had dinner on time.

However, in the standard case CI does not behave like material implication. We shall represent CI by

(p > q), i.e. 'p counterfactually implies q'.

The most influential attempt to this day at giving a semantics for counterfactuals is the classical 'possible world approach' due to Stalnaker [1968] and Lewis [1973]. The intuition of that approach runs as follows: we shall consider a sentence such as S1 as true, if we can imagine a course of events W such that

(i) the electricity didn't fail;
(ii) otherwise, W is as close as possible to the actual course of events;
(iii) W must itself be consistent;
(iv) in the imagined course of events W, we did have dinner on time.

Requirement (ii) forestalls the introduction of completely arbitrary changes which cause the consequence S3 to become true; for instance, it may become true by our ordering some ready-made dinner, which arrives on time. But for the entire CI to be true, the consequence must become true 'on account of the antecedent's becoming true'. Requirement (iii) reflects the fact that to construe the desired alternative course of events, it is not sufficient simply to assume the truth of S2; for instance, in the actual course of events there may be some fact, say

(S4) The local power plant broke down this afternoon.

which entails the falsity of S2. Then we would have to assume the falsity of S4 in order to consistently assume the truth of S2. Finally, requirement (iv) has deliberately been formulated in a somewhat loose manner, since Stalnaker and Lewis differ on this point. Stalnaker merely requires that there be *some* such course of events, in which we did have dinner on time, whereas Lewis requires that we have dinner on time in *all* such 'worlds' in order for the CI to be true. (iv) may be reformulated into one or the other direction.

The classical possible worlds approach was summarized and refined by M. L. Ginsberg [1986]. We shall state how the above intuitions can be formalized using Ginsberg reconstruction of the classical approach:

The semantics is based on a triple $(W, F, <_F)$ such that
- W is a set of possible worlds. In the classical approach, these are construed as sets of propositions.
- F is a fixed world (which may be considered to be the actual world).
- $<_F$ is a partial ordering on W such that
for all U, V in W: $U <_F V$ iff
'V is at least as similar to F as U'.
In its simplest form, $<_F$ is the partial ordering induced by set inclusion on the powerset of F.

Now consider a counterfactual $(p > q)$, where p is known to be false, i.e. $(F \models \sim p)$. Loosely speaking, in order to establish the truth of $(p > q)$ we need to (1) consider those possible worlds U such that p can be true in U, i.e. $(U \not\models \sim p)$, but which are otherwise 'maximally similar to F', and (2) see whether those worlds satisfy the implication $(p => q)$. So the underlying intuition is that for instance S1 should be regarded as true, if it can be shown that we would indeed have dinner on time in any world where the electricity didn't fail, but which is otherwise as similar as possible to the actual world.

This is captured by the following definitions:

- the set of possible worlds for p in F, $M(p,F)$, is given by

$$M(p, F) = \{V \subseteq F \mid (V \not\models \neg p) \land (\forall T [(V \subset T \subseteq F) \rightarrow (T \vdash \neg p)])\}$$

It may be noted that the righthand side of the conjunct is the maximality requirement in its simplest form, namely that of plain set inclusion.

- truth condition for CI:

$$\|(p>q)\|(F) = 1 \quad \text{iff} \quad \forall T \in M(p, F) : \|(p \rightarrow q)\|(T) = 1$$

Observe that $M(p,F) = \{F\}$ for $(F \models p)$, so the construction makes CI and material implication coincide whenever the antecedent of the CI is actually true.

Finally, we should mention one salient property of CI, which is extensively discussed in most papers on the subject, namely that of *non-monotonicity*.

Material implication is monotonic, a fact which may be rendered by the formula

$$(*)\ (p => q) => ((p \,\&\, r) => q).$$

In classical logic, (*) is a valid formula. Not so for CI. For instance, the truth of S1 does not entail the truth of

(S5)   If the electricity hadn't failed, and the cook had refused to prepare the dinner, we would have had dinner on time.

In other words, the CI-analogue of (*),

$$(\#)\ (p > q) => ((p \,\&\, r) > q)$$

is not a valid formula. This property is also captured within the classical approach.

2. Text-dependent properties of counterfactuals

The classical approach has not acquired its fame without reason. It is intuitively appealing and formally well understood (at least if we ignore the problems with giving a more adequate formalization of the 'maximal similarity requirement'). Nevertheless, it seems to us that the classical approach misses out on a very basic semantic property: the dynamical dependency of CI on information in the surrounding text. To see this, let us consider one piece of text (written for this purpose). It should be noted that the example is directed towards a certain class of CI's, namely those which may be interpreted in terms of 'causation'. The reason for this is quite practical: the implementation CIMP, which will be discussed below, was designed for studies in causal reasoning rather than Automated text understanding or counterfactual implication in general. Of course, this means a slight loss of generality in the discussion, but it gains us the merit of discussing in relation to an actual implementation. Now the story:

> Joe wants to invite some of his friends for dinner. He goes to the local grocer's to buy the ingredients, and he hires a cook, who is supposed to prepare the meal. The cook arrives at Joe's house, but he finds that there is an electrical failure, which will make it impossible to prepare the dinner in due time. Now a discussion of a rather hypothetical nature evolves between Joe and his friend Jim.
> Joe: If it had not been for the failure, we would have had dinner on time. (A)
> Jim: You're wrong. If the cook had left, you might not have had dinner on time, even in the absence of the failure. (B)

> Joe: Well, I was just assuming that the cook would stay. But what I mean is that if there were no failure and the cook agreed to stay, we would have had dinner on time. (C)
> Jim: You're wrong again. If you had not been to the grocer's to buy the ingredients, you might not have had dinner on time, even if the cook had agreed to stay and no electrical failure had occurred. (D)
> Joe: Nevertheless, even if I had not procured the ingredients, we would have had dinner on time, if I had ordered some ready-made dinner instead. (E)

It goes on and on like that for several more pages, but we shall end our example here. To our minds, the crucial feature of the above discussion is the fact that each successive and apparently contradictory counterfactual statement should be considered as true at the respective 'stages' of the discussion. In other words, they are true with respect to the information in the text which is being taken into consideration when each statement is made. Of course, the apparent change in truth values has to do with the non-monotonicity of CI, a property which is also captured at a general level within the classical approach. However, once a Ginsberg model has been specified, each of the statements will be evaluated as true or false 'once and for all'. The inherent dynamics of the text is not reflected within the classical approach, where CI is simply conceived as a relation between an antecedent and a consequence. The above example, however, calls for a third argument in the evaluation of CI's, namely an argument reflecting what information is being taken into account. Indeed, we may interpret the discussion as being concerned with what information should be taken into account rather than a discussion of the actual truth-or-falsity of specific CI's. The point is that there is always a *ceteris paribus* clause involved in counterfactual statements and statements concerning causality. This clause determines which possible courses of events should be taken into consideration in order to evaluate the statement in question. So this extra argument of the counterfactual or causality predicate defines the set of entities relevant for the evaluation of the statement. We shall call this the *scope* of the statement. Before we describe how we may actually implement our revised notion of causal and counterfactual implication, it should be useful to present an alternative setting within which CI can be discussed, namely that of branching time.

3. Branching Time

Another piece of criticism of the classical approach is the observation that it does not pay sufficient attention to the rôle of time and tense in counterfactual arguments. That observation is at the heart of Shoham's work on counterfactuals, as can be seen in for instance [Shoham 1990]. In fairness it must be said that this deficiency becomes particularly obvious exactly when it comes to *causal* CI's, a subclass with which the classical analysis was not particularly concerned. On the other hand, it is also clear that time and tense play a rôle in connection with CI in general, even at the syntactical level. The kind of temporal logic most suited for the discussion of CI is the class of systems known as 'branching time'. We may illustrate a BT-model for the story above as follows (slightly simplified for the purpose of exposition):

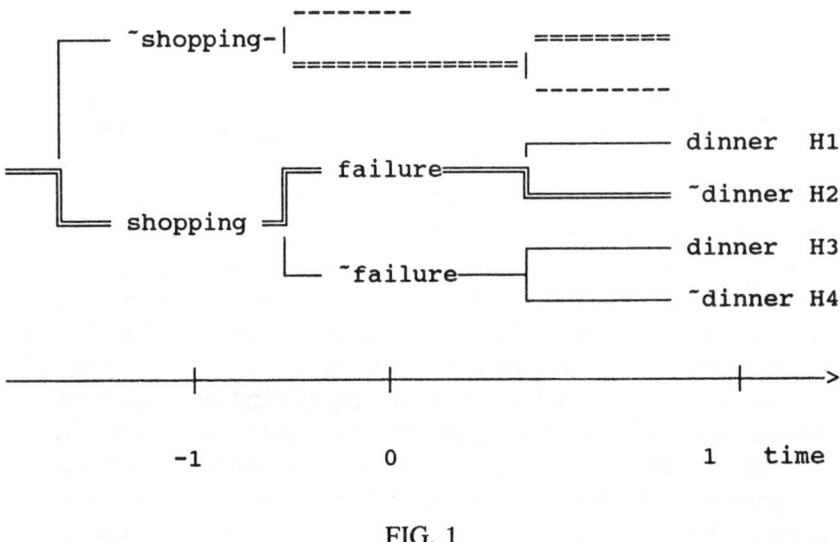

FIG. 1

This branching time tree-structure provides us with a model for our short story, that is, it can serve as a basis for evaluating the (A) - (E) statements (for the sake of simplicity, *ingredients* and *cook* have been left out of the picture). We can make a number of important distinctions based on this model.

Before doing so we should like to make one general remark, though: in this paper, we are concerned with general principles and ideas rather than technical details. The exposition is adapted accordingly. However, those interested in the technicalities can find them in [Øhrstrøm, Hasle, and Pedersen 1992], where a BT-based formal semantics for counterfactuals has been stated in detail. In that paper we have also given a much more detailed account of the proof-theory, the proof-strategy, and the semantics of the CIMP-program. Let us now turn to the distinctions based on our BT-model: The 'highlighted' branch H2 corresponds to the actual 'history' assumed in the story. We call this the *true history*. All of the histories H1 - H4 are the *possible histories* expanding under the node *shopping*. Given that H2 is the 'true history', H1, H3 and H4 can aptly be called *counterfactual histories*. Furthermore, some of the possible histories may be ruled out by underlying causal assumptions in the text. It can be argued that in our story, it is tacitly assumed that if Joe has done his shopping and there is no electrical failure, then we shall in fact have dinner on time. In that case H4 is effectively ruled out. We shall call the possible histories which are not ruled out the *permissible histories* (in our case, H1 - H3). The dotted lines expanding under *~shopping* are also in a certain sense counterfactual histories, but taking '0' for the 'now' they can no longer be regarded as possible - this circumstance is sometimes referred to as the asymmetry between a fixed past and an open future (see the Lewis-quote below). Even so, we can talk about a *preferred history*, illustrated by double dotted lines. In general, we need a selection function which for any state in the BT-system can give us a preferred history, but here we shall leave out that technical detail. Finally, it should be mentioned that the numbers on the time line need not be regarded strictly as clock time, or instants for that matter. Intuitively, they can be seen as names of relevant time intervals into which the progress of events can be subdivided.

An adequate evaluation procedure for our (A) - (E) statements can now be suggested: in each statement, a number of causal factors are being taken into consideration. To evaluate the statement, we can construe a tree consisting of all permissible histories (if no specific causal assumptions are taken into account, this will simply be the tree of all possible histories). Then, the counterfactual implication (p > q) can be evaluated as true, if q holds in all permissible histories in which the antecedent p holds, and false otherwise.

Generally speaking, the BT-model is a basis for a tempo-modal language, in which formulas such as

(i) $F(1)\sim$dinner
(ii) POSSIBLY $(F(1)$dinner$)$
(iii) $P(2)$ (POSSIBLY$(F(1)\sim$shopping$))$

are meaningful. A bare future statement such as (i) is true iff it holds in the true history (H2) - (i) may be read as saying that in one time unit ahead of the assumed 'now' (0), the dinner won't be ready. (ii) may be read as saying that there is a permissible history H such that in H, the dinner will be ready in one time unit from now. The formula (iii) indicates that we may also so to speak work ourselves backwards in the structure, and from there reach other courses of events, which failed to ever materialize (indicated by the dotted lines in figure 1). The temporal logic sketched here is a metrical tense logic. It may be noted that a proposition without any explicit indication of time, e.g. *failure* in the formula

$$failure \Rightarrow F(1)\sim dinner$$

is understood to refer to the 'now'. (It may indeed be argued that this ability of having explicitly tensed formulas alongside with 'untensed' formulas is one of the principal virtues of tense logic - see the discussion in [Hasle 1991]).

Of course, much more could be said about BT formalisms. The assumption of a true history, which stretches into the future, is but one of the various BT systems. A useful overview of BT systems can be found in [Øhrstrøm 1988]. As for the intimate connection between BT and CI, it should be mentioned that this was observed already by Lewis himself, who summarized the relation as follows:

> The past would be the same, however we acted now. The past does not at all depend on what we do now. It is counterfactually independent of the present...I suggest that the mysterious asymmetry between open future and fixed past is nothing else than the asymmetry of counterfactual dependence. The forking paths [within a BT structure] into the future - the actual one and all the rest - are the many alternative futures that would come about under various counterfactual suppositions about the present. The one actual, fixed past is the one past that would remain actual under this same range of suppositions. (Lewis 1979, p. 462)

4. CIMP - a Sketch of the Implementation

CIMP is a Prolog program for evaluating *C*ounterfactual *Imp*lication. At the virtual level, it may be described as operating essentially on three databases:

(i) CAUSAL - a database which holds the assumed basic causal relations;
(ii) ACTUAL - a list of all the propositions assumed to be actually true (i.e. the true history);
(iii) RULES - the non-classical logical rules specifically designed for the evaluation of causal counterfactuals.

An important fourth component is, of course, the inference engine 'running' the three components above.

Our short story obviously assumes one basic causal relation, which may be depicted like this:

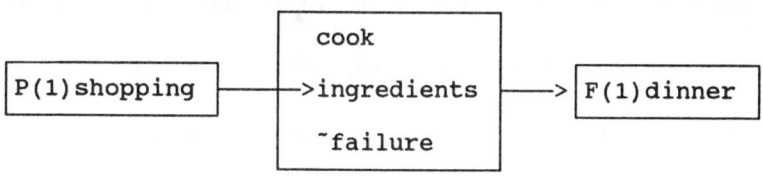

FIG. 2

This basic causal relation also underlies Joe's and Jim's respective arguments. *P(1)shopping* is a sufficient cause of *ingredients*. However, *ingredients* is not by itself a sufficient cause of *F(1)dinner*, but on the other hand it is a necessary part of the causal complex for *F(1)dinner*. For this reason the invidual constituents of a causal complex for an effect E are called '*I*nsufficient but *N*ecessary parts of an *U*nnecessary but *S*ufficient' cause of E - in short, they are INUS conditions (cf. [Mackie 1974]). The complex in its entirety is called 'unnecessary' due to the fact that there may be other sufficient causes of E - for instance, that we have ordered some ready-made dinner, which arrives on time. We shall represent such causality relations by predicates of the form

causal(SCOPE,CAUSAL_COMPLEX,EFFECT).

The SCOPE reflects which factors are being taken into account in statements made at various 'stages' of the text. So our causal-predicate captures the kind of three-place relation that we previously argued was needed for evaluating CI's in general. All propositions occurring in the scope list should be unnegated, since the SCOPE simply lists what propositions are considered as relevant, not whether they are actually true or not. So the causal database corresponding to figure 2 would be:

causal([P(1)shopping,ingredients],   /* SCOPE */
   [P(1)shopping],   /* CAUSAL_COMPLEX */
   ingredients).   /* EFFECT */

causal([cook,ingredients,failure,F(1)dinner], /* S */
   [cook,ingredients,~failure],   /* C */
   F(1)dinner).   /* E */

The actual course of events, that is, the true history, is simply rendered by

actual([P(1)shopping,cook,ingredients,failure,F(1)~dinner]).

By extension, we shall also say that this clause entails *actual(p)* for any p in the list.

As for the special rules for evaluating CI, we shall mention but three:

(R1) If causal([p1,p2,...,pN],[q1,q2,...,qM],e) is included in the causal database, then
scope([p1,p2,...,pN]): (q1 & q2 & ... & qM) > e

- this rule simply tells how to 'read off' a CI from the causal database.

(R2) 'Causal Cut':
    (a) scope([p1,p2,...,pN]): (q1 & q2 & ... & qM) > e
    (b) (q1 & q2 & ... & qM) |- e => d

    (c) scope([p1,p2,...,pN]): (q1 & q2 & ... & qM) > d

- where all literals occurring in e and d are included in scope([p1,p2,...,pN]).

(R3) 'Causal Restriction':
    (a) scope([p1,p2,...,pN,r]): (q1 & q2 & ... & qM & r) > e
    (b) actual(r)

    (c) scope([p1,p2,...,pN]): (q1 & q2 & ... & qM) > e

- this rule is vital for 'diminishing' the CI's of the causal database in a manner which is sensitive to the information being taken into account at various stages of the text. Thus the rule implements the previously discussed *ceteris paribus* assumption of counterfactual arguments. (As it stands here, (R3) might under certain circumstances introduce inconsistency, so we shall assume that it is subject to suitable consistency constraints. However, these are not important to the examples discussed below.)

Observe that the logical forms occurring in these rules suggest that a CI is always evaluated with respect to a given scope. The use of such rules also indicates a proof-theoretical way of evaluating counterfactuals, whereas the previous discussion of BT suggested a semantical way of doing things. In practice, CIMP combines both approaches to proving theorems, as is common in logic programming.

5. Application of CIMP to Counterfactuals - Some Examples

On the premises outlined above, how can we go about evaluating the (A) - (E) statements of our text? First of all it should be noted that the actual- and causal-databases corresponding to our text have here been extracted manually. Therefore, if we relate our examples to the ultimate goal of automated text understanding, namely *fully* automated text analysis, it must be said that the

CIMP algorithm presupposes the existence of a system already capable of extracting this kind of databases.

In order to evaluate the (A) statement, we need to stipulate a suitable formal representation for it. In the logical language suggested above, that representation could be

(1)   scope([failure,F(1)dinner)]):
      ~failure > F(1)dinner.

By inspecting the causal-database in accordance with (R1), we immediately have

(2)   scope([cook,ingredients,failure,F(1)dinner]):
      (cook & ingredients & ~failure) > F(1)dinner.

The natural strategy now is to try to reduce (2) into (1). This can indeed be done using successive applications of *causal restriction*: as a first step, we may 'delete' the factor *cook*, for our actual-database entails

(3)   actual(cook),

and according to R3 this yields together with (2):

(4)   scope([ingredients,failure,F(1)dinner]):
      (ingredients & ~failure) > F(1)dinner.

In a similar manner, we can do away with *ingredients* (of course, in the implementation all these reductions are carried out in one fell swoop). We then obtain

(5)   scope([failure,F(1)dinner]):
      ~failure > F(1)dinner.

which is identical to (1) - that is, we have proved the truth of the counterfactual implication. As it is described here the procedure would appear to be entirely deductive. However, we also could have constructed the BT-tree for (1), which we have already seen (as a major subtree of figure 1). Then, we would have had a semantical proof of (1), since the implication

(~failure) => F(1)dinner

holds in all permissible histories, in which the antecedents holds.

Let us now turn to the (B) statement. Since the sentence contains the modal auxiliary 'might', we shall stipulate the representation

(6)   scope([cook,ingredients,F(1)dinner]):
       M((~cook & ~failure) > F(1)~dinner)

where M is to be read 'possibly'.

Since the scope is broader more histories should be taken into consideration. The possible histories w.r.t. the scope in question are

H1.   [cook,failure,F(1)dinner]
H2.   [cook,~failure,F(1)dinner]
H3.   [cook,failure,F(1)~dinner]
H4.   [cook,~failure,F(1)~dinner]
H5.   [~cook,failure,F(1)dinner]
H6.   [~cook,~failure,F(1)dinner]
H7.   [~cook,failure,F(1)~dinner]
H8.   [~cook,~failure,F(1)~dinner]

The history H4, however, violates our causal assumptions and hence is not permissible. But at any rate, only H6 and H8 are relevant for evaluating (6), since they are the only ones to satisfy the antecedent. Now the possibility-operator suggests that all that is required for evaluating (6) as true is that there be *some* permissible history satisfying the implication

(~cook & ~failure) => F(1)~dinner.

Clearly, H8 fulfills that requirement. One might ask what would happen if we dropped the modal auxiliary, respectively the possibility operator, in our current example. At the intuitive level, it does not seem unnatural to have Jim saying simply

> You're wrong. If the cook had left, you would not have had dinner on time, even in the absence of the failure. (B')

(and believing in the truth of this statement). Nevertheless, we think that (B') should be evaluated as false. The causal assumptions discussed so far do not specify a set of conditions leading infallibly to *F(1)~dinner* - and that is what would be required for us to truthfully assert any 'non-modal' statement of the form

p > F(1)~dinner.

(B') could be true only if our causal model explicitly contained a complex with *F(1)~dinner* as the effect, such as

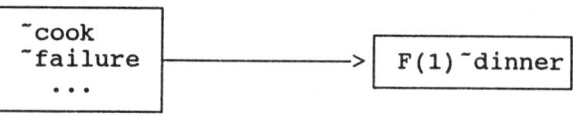

FIG. 3

The (C) and (D) statements are evaluated in a manner analogous to (A) and (B), respectively. So let us turn to our final example, the (E) statement. Our examples so far should have served to demonstrate how CI's should be evaluated depending on what we have been calling the 'scope'. The (E) statement, however, will show how a general change of the information in the text should be reflected by changes in our databases, thus reflecting a change induced by the dynamics of the text itself. The point is that the (E) statement introduces a new causal relation, which changes the picture of the causal-database as follows:

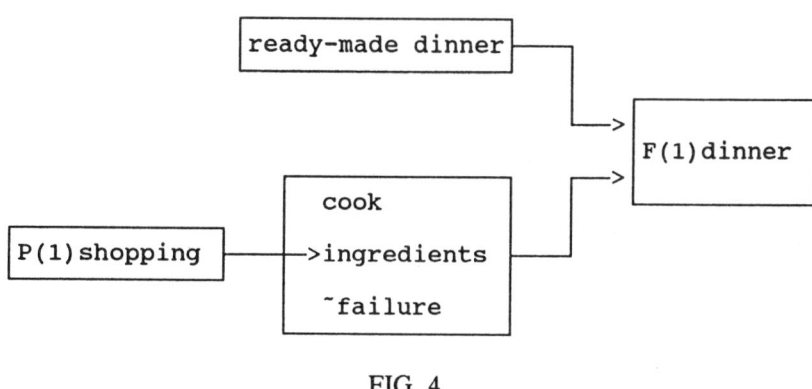

FIG. 4

Of course, the causal-database is to be updated accordingly by the introduction of an extra causal-predicate clause. To maintain a complete database, we must also add

$\sim$ready-made-dinner

to the actual-database (to make it clear that in the true history, Joe did *not* order any ready-made dinner).

Now we may represent the (E) statement as

($\sim$ingredients & ready-made-dinner) > F(1)dinner.

No possibility operator is required here, for all permissible histories actually satisfying *ready-made-dinner* will also satisfy *F(1)dinner* - in short, the (E) statement evaluates to true.

6. Conclusion

The treatment of counterfactual implication in this paper differs from the classical approach in some important respects. The major formal expression of these differences is the representation of CI-relations as three-place predicates. The underlying idea is that such relations should always be interpreted with respect to a given context. That context defines not only what we have called the scope, but also a set of assumptions which enter into the evaluation process. In the case of CIMP, we have been concerned with *causal* assumptions, but in principle a wide range of relevance relations may well be amenable to a similar treatment. One major advantage of our treatment is the fact that no notion of 'maximal similarity' is required - a notion, which has proved to be most troublesome for the classical approach to the semantics of CI. On the other hand, this advantage is gained at the cost of having to specify explicitly some of the information otherwise implicit in the text (or context). The requirement that this information has somehow already been specified is the main limitation to the potential use of our treatment within Automated text understanding. Nevertheless, the properties of our treatment seem to us to be more adequate for the purposes of Automated text understanding than is the classical approach. Automated text understanding systems must be capable of doing many things; one of them is to deal with counterfactuals. To that extent the results of this paper may be seen simply as contributing just one of the many bits and pieces required for the development of Automated text understanding.

However, the close relation between CI and BT may suggest that these issues are of a more general importance for Automated text understanding. Surely the temporal structure of a text is one of the main factors in the text understanding process, be it human or mechanical. As we have just suggested, we may see the above investigation as being concerned with how to evaluate CI's against a textual background. Alternatively, we may see it as a progressive representation of some of the dynamical aspects of a text in terms of branching time and counterfactual relations. From that perspective, the investigation may serve to illustrate how BT may be used for more general purposes within Automated text understanding.

7. Acknowledgements

The work contained in this paper has been carried out under a grant from the Framework Programme in Cognitive Science under the Danish Research Council for the Humanities.

References

Ginsberg, M. L. (1986) *Counterfactuals*, Artificial Intelligence 30.

Hasle, Per (1991) 'Building a Temporal Logic for NLU with the HOL-system' in: C. Brown and G. Kock (eds), *Natural Language Understanding and Logic Programming* 3, pp. 92-110, North Holland, Dordrecht.

Lewis, David (1973) *Counterfactuals*. Harvard University Press, Cambridge MA.

Lewis, David (1979) *Counterfactual Dependence and Time's Arrow*. in: NOUS 13, pp. 455-476.

Mackie, J. L. (1974) *The Cement of the Universe: A Study in Causation*, Oxford University Press.

Shoham, Yoav (1990) *Nonmonotonic Reasoning and Causation*, Cognitive Science 14, pp. 213-252.

Stalnaker, R. (1968) 'A theory of conditionals' in: N. Rescher (ed), *Studies in Logical Theory*. Oxford University Press, Oxford.

Øhrstrøm, Peter, Per Hasle and Stig Andur Pedersen (In print) 'Logical Models of Causal and Temporal Reasoning', in: *Proceedings of the Second MOHAWC Workshop*, Bamberg 1991. Risø National Laboratory, Roskilde.

Øhrstrøm, Peter (1988) 'Problems Regarding the Future Operator in an Indeterministic Tense Logic' in: Peter Øhrstrøm: *Nogle Aspekter af tidsbegrebets rolle i de eksakte videnskaber med særligt henblik på logikken*, pp. 106 - 115. Aalborg Universitetsforlag. (Dr. Scient. afhandling).

Cognitive Grammar and Text Understanding

Inger Lytje
Aalborg University

1. Introduction

Natural language understanding is an important subfield of artificial intelligence focusing on computer modelling of natural language (Lytje 1992). The issue of computer modelling has primarily been studied from a computational linguistics point of view, focusing on computer implementation of formal linguistic theory within a generative and logical paradigm (Allen 1987). As early as the late seventies, Terry Winograd and others pointed out that the generative paradigm has been confused with the computational paradigm (Winograd 1980, 1983). Within a computational paradigm the computer is considered an information processing device that manipulat symbols according to some regularity: "The computer shares with the human mind the ability to manipulate symbols and carry out complex processes that include making decisions on the basis of stored knowledge" (Winograd 1983, p.13). These ideas have primarily been explored from a cognitive science perspective focusing on the issue of understanding. From this perspective language is dealt with at discourse level rather than sentence level, and the main interest concerns language as knowledge.

From a cognitive science point of view it has been critisized that knowledge and reasoning have been considered synonymous with logic(Schank & Abelson 1987), and researchers in cognitive science and artificial intelligence have pointed at other knowledge structures, the most radical being neural networks.

In this paper I will discuss computer modelling within a computational paradigm regarding the computer as an information processing device that can be used as an experimental research tool in linguistics and cognitive science. Language understanding is considered a cognitive process that is formed by linguistic structure, and I want to study the interaction between cognitive process and linguistic structure. So my point of departure is language use rather than language system, and that has led me to consider the problem of text comprehension.

Cognitive linguistics integrates a linguistic and a cognitive perspective on language understanding. This acknowledgement has led me into Ronald Langackers theory of cognitive grammar(Langacker 1987, 1990). The theory focuses on the relation between grammar and language use and on the relation between linguistic and extra linguistic knowledge. Langacker does not even mention the issue of computer modelling. Yet I believe that his cognitive linguistic theory can be applied to natural language understanding. It

Steen Jansen et al (eds): Computational Approaches to Text Understanding,
© Museum Tusculanum Press, Copenhagen 1992

comprises a comprehensive formalization of the processes of the mind that may function as a basis for implementations of computer simulations.

The perspective of making experiments with computer modelling according to cognitive linguistic theory is both scientific and technological. From a scientific point of view, computer modelling implies that the theory can be evaluated from an empirical point of view and the results from the computation can be used to enlighten the process of language understanding. From a technological point of view it will result in enhancement of the quality of linguistic engineering products.

2. Text comprehension and artificial intelligence

In the following I will refer to some of the results from artificial intelligence and cognitive science concerning computer modelling of text comprehension. Schank & Abelson's book, *Scripts Plans and Goals* (Schank & Abelson 1977) is considered a classic within the field. Furthermore I will refer to Jerry Hobbs from Stanford Research Institute and his work on discourse analyses (Hobbs 1990). Despite their different backgrounds and approaches, there are many common features in their way of considering the problem. One of the most significant is their focus on coherence and inference structure. How does it come about that a text is considered coherent in our minds despite the lack of literal expression of coherence relations in the text.

Schank & Abelson have been working with story understanding which, at the knowledge level, is considered a sequence of coherent events. The inference structure such as causality, that make the event sequence coherent, are not always represented literally in the text. To understand means to be able to make the inference structures explicit. This ability is established by using an information structure called a script. Scripts are considered psychologically real, and they make it possible for us to cope with predictable situations in everyday life according to routine. Script structures are very similar to Lakoffs image schemas (Lakoff 1987) and some of the semantic structures proposed by Langacker (Langacker 1987). The criteria for understanding a story, according to Schank & Abelson, is that the computer is able to translate the story into a semantic structure based on conceptual dependency formulas and using scripts as a knowledge base. The conceptual dependency formula shows explicitly the event structure of the story. In order to demonstrate the idea they have developed a computer program SAM which is able to understand simple stories. Within artificial intelligence, scripts have been seen as an alternative to logic as a knowledge representation scheme.

In his book *Literature and Cognition* Jerry R. Hobbs presents a theory of discourse interpretation, suggesting four types of coherence relations: occasion, evaluation, figure-ground and expanson and comprising the interpretation of metaphor (Hobbs 1990). Hobbs suggests that meaning is to be understood as interpretation, and I find the formula $F(K,T)=I$ (Hobbs 1990 p.20) very useful as a basis for thinking about text comprehension. The formula says that the interpretation process is formed partly by the reader's belief system (K for knowledge system) and partly by the literal text (T for text), and that it results in an interpretation I which (rather loosely) is considered "some formal representation of the content of the text" which ".. encodes the information conveyed by the text, the relevant inferences and the implicit structural relations" (Hobbs 1990 p.23).

The formula opens two conceptions of text comprehension. The one is that the belief system of the reader is changed as a result of reading and understanding a text; the text restructures processes in mind and body, making it a subjective process of acknowledgement. The other is that the inference structures of the text are made explicit using the belief system K similar to Shank & Abelsons ideas of making inference structures explicit. I think that both conceptions should be considered. The formula also stresses the importance of the hermeneutical circle according to which meaning emerges differently in every reading, because a reading changes our belief system.

According to J. Hobbs, understanding a text means translating the text sentence by sentence into logical form. Furthermore he suggests that discourse structure is built recursively from the semantic structure of single clauses being linked by coherence relations that are identified from the conceptual structures of the clauses involved. As mentioned above, understanding depends on knowledge, and Hobbs suggests that knowledge is stored as axioms in a knowledge base, expressing the agent's ability to make inferences. So Hobbs chooses formal logic as semantic structure.

3. Comprehension, cognition and computation

In the preceeding paragraph we have refered to two semantic theories, conceptual dependency and predicate logic. I will consider conceptual dependency an event grammar that can only be used to analyze stories. Moreover conceptual dependency theory only deals with literal meaning and not with metaphor, which is now considered pervasive not only in figurative language but in language use in general. On the other hand there is a similarity between the use of scripts and cognitive semantic theory, although the label cognitive semantics was not invented in the 1970'ties. The script structure is cognitively motivated and open to computer implementation.

As mentioned above, predicate logic is a very pervasive semantic theory in computational linguistics, and it has been implemented in many systems. Despite the successes, there still reside computational problems that seem very hard to overcome. They stem from the fact that the theory does not account for the variation in the meaning of linguistic expression. And the reason for that has to be found in the principles of categorization. Langacker states it in the following way: "it cannot in general be presumed that membership in a linguistic category is a predictable all-or-nothing affair" (Langacker

1987 p.369). The separation of syntax and semantics implies that semantic interpretation is considered a translation relation between syntactic and semantic structure. This translation problem has been a major research area in computational linguistics for many years, but the computational problems seem very hard to overcome. I think that the problems that appear as technological problems come from deficiences in the theoretical foundation.

This acknowledgement has made me consider Langackers theory of cognitive grammar as a theoretical foundation of computer modelling of text comprehension. Accordingly I conceive text comprehension as a mental process that is formed by a cognitive grammar, and which recognizes semantic structures in a text and their interrelationships. The computer simulation of this process is called semantic parsing. It is still unclear to me to what extent the resulting semantic structure will be open to interpretation, but further experiments will show that.

4. Computer modelling based on cognitive grammar

Cognitive linguistic theory does not immediately inform us about how to build computer models of natural language understanding. It does not even provide a written grammar for any language that could be used as a starting point for formalization. The theory regards language as a cognitive process, and it describes in a detailed and formalized manner the link between linguistic structure and the cognitive processes that constitute understanding. Meaning is considered mental imagery. It means that the same situation can call on different, images dependent on the features that are selected, the degree of abstractness and the perspective. Using the computer as a metaphor for the mind within an AI tradition, we find many very detailed guidelines concerning computer modelling in Langackers theory. In the following we will look into some of the crucial ones.

4.1. Categorization

Langacker stresses the importance of categorization to language understanding. Linguistic entities are analyzed in terms of complex categories. Similar to other cognitive linguists, Langacker finds that classical categories do not capture the facts of linguistic knowledge. Instead he suggests a category model based on the notion of schematicity comprising both full schematicity and partial schematicity. Through a categorizing judgement the schema is instantiated (elaborated), matching the schema specifications, which represent generality, to a specialized instance of the schema. The schema is referred to as a prototype if the categorizing judgement involves extension (instead of mere elaboration) in order to get a match between general specifications and an instant. To illustrate the idea of extension consider Hobbs' example of the term "plow" in "the ship plows through the water"(Hobbs 1990 p.55). Usually the medium for plowing is earth, but in order to understand the sentence we have to abstract from that and only consider more abstract features such as linear motion in a straight line. In this case it makes it possible to transfer the meaning of "plow" from its literal sense to metaphor.

Let us observe the category structure of a lexicon (Langacker p. 370) and the implications concerning computer modelling. The whole lexicon is regarded as a schematic network. The variety of meanings of a lexical item results from extensions of the same prototype or different instantiations of the same schema. Moreover a lexicon is considered a dynamic body of knowledge in the sense that the categories are elaborated and extended through language use and learning. By enlarging the vocabulary and by increasing and modifying the categorizing relationships the system's linguistic competence and knowledge will be enhanced.

A lexicon can be represented in a computer using frame structures (Rich 1983; Vasey & Westwood 1990), which seem to cope with the variety of meanings in a natural way. In classical systems the problem of multiple meanings is usually handled by entering all possible meanings of a specific lexical item in the lexicon. This approach has three deficiencies. First, the number of meanings is in principle infinite, so which ones and how many of the infinitely many meanings should be entered? Second, the approach causes a problem of complexity during computation of linguistic structure because there are so many possibilities of combinations. And third, different meanings usually are related, and this fact cannot be represented.

Because of the symbolic nature of linguistic knowledge (see below) the semantic space of a lexicon can be seen as a knowledge base. From the point of view that knowledge is symbolic, the lexicon will be the only knowledge base in a computer model. This knowledge base is formatted as a frame based system as opposed to a rule based system.

4.2. Grammar

According to Langacker and according to European linguistic tradition, syntax and semantics need not be regarded as separate components of a grammar. They are considered the two sides of the linguistic symbol, and a grammar is considered a structured inventory of symbolic units. According to Langacker, a symbol has a phonological and a semantic pole, and each of the poles are considered complex categories, that are cognitively motivated: "Lexicon and grammar are storehouses of conventional imagery.." (Langacker 1987 p.47).

It has been emphasized above that according to a classical computational linguistics paradigm, semantic structure is computed from syntactical structure. Moreover it has been emphasized that this translation process is a very critical one, both from a computational and from a conceptual point of view. According to a cognitive grammar, phonological structure and semantic structure are parallel in many significant respects. Therefore information at the semantic pole can immediately be derived from information obtained at the phonological pole. We need no translation. So there are reasons to believe that the symbolic conception of meaning will make us overcome one of the most critical aspects of natural language understanding systems.

Valency relations are the cognitive linguistic parallel to grammar rules. Valency is considered a quality inherent to the linguistic symbol. It informs us about the potential connections that the symbol can have to other linguistic symbols. And it tells us how the meaning of a complex symbol is derived from the meaning of its parts. So valency is considered a feature inherent to linguistic symbols.

In relation to computer modelling, valency relations have implications for the formation of parsing strategies. Langacker goes through four factors that he finds important to valency relations (Langacker p.277), and I find that especially the principle of profile determinacy and the principle of conceptual autonomy and dependency are of utmost importance to computer modelling. According to the first one, the profile of a complex linguistic expression is enherited from the profile of one of its components in a regular manner. For example a football is a ball and a blackbird is a bird. According to the other principle, some predications are autonomous and some are dependent. Usually, the dependent predications are relational and the autonomous predications are nominal (thing). This observation points at a mechanism which may regulate the parsing process. As an example we can consider the phrase "the conference in Copenhagen". "in" symbolizes a relational predication (a container relation). "in" is considered a dynamic object, and it "wants to" have its trajector and landmark elaborated. It succeeds in doing so by capturing "the conference" as trajector and "Copenhagen" as landmark. Using the principle of profile determinacy, the resulting semantic structure is a thing category, namely "the conference". In a larger context this category may enter into a relation at a higher level of complexity, elaborating another trajector or landmark schema of another relational predication.

To summarize, we can conclude that the parsing process is not a rule based process, but runs by interaction between linguistic entities which enter into asymmetric trajector landmark relations. The process goes from bottom up, starting with morphemes which enter into still more complex linguistic symbols. This points at object oriented programming and parallellism, and it points at a computer model, attaching semantic and processual information to linguistic objects. Concerning the resulting semantic structure, it emerges as a recursive network built from embedded trajector-landmark relations, the lowest level being a thing that is symbolized by a morpheme.

As an example regard the sentense "Flaget blafrer i vinden" ("the flag is fluttering in the wind"). It will be analyzed into the following semantic network:

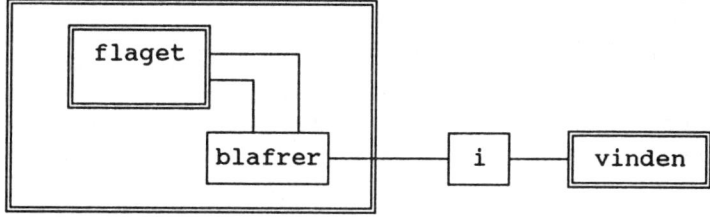

Fig. 1

4.3. Lexicon and morphology

Langacker's claim, that basic grammatical categories are semantically definable, is extensively used in our computer model. Figure 2 below shows the semantic parallel to the word classes. Some of them are defined using semantic structure, and others, conjunction and article, are defined by functionality.

CORRESPONDENCE BETWEEN WORD CLASS AND
SEMANTIC STRUCTURE

WORD	SEMANTIC STRUCTURE
Verb	Process
Noun	Thing
Adjective	Relation between a thing and a place on some scale
Adverb	Relation between relation and a place in some space
Preposition	Spatial relation between two entities
Pronoun	Thing
Conjunction	Sequencing of entities
Article	Selection of entities
Numeral	Relation between a thing and a place on the number scale
Interjection	

Fig. 2

Grammatical categories are characterized by schemas that are compatible with all the members of the category it defines. In the following we will go into the verb schema, the noun schema and the relational schema corresponding to adverbs, adjectives and prepositions. All the schemas describe a word stem morpheme. Affixes are dependent morphemes that are appended to word stems, symbolizing semantic function in the sense that the meaning of the composite structure can be derived from the meaning of the participating morphemes.

The semantic structure of a verb is a process, and according to Langacker, processes are characterized by having a temporal profile: "the conceptualization of a process follows the temporal evolution of a situation. It involves a continuous series of states representing different phases of the process and construed as occupying a continuous series of points in conceived time" (p.244). Accordingly verbs may occur in present tense, past tense and present and past participle. The verb schema has a feature that contains the morphemes that symbolize the tenses and also the morphemes that symbolize change in profile e.g. from process to thing. Another feature contains purely semantic information concerning the relation and the process that the verb symbolizes. In our experimental computer model the possible values of purely semantic features are shown in figure 3 below:

VERB

FEATURE VALUE	RELATION PROTOTYPE
Action	Relation between two physical objects
Intrans	Motion or state in space / Natural process
Cognition	Mental process
Communication	Goal oriented process
Auxilary	

Fig. 3

The semantic structure of a noun is a thing. Langacker conceives a thing as "a region being profiled in some domain", and he stresses that "we ..cannot account for meaning by describing objective reality, but only by describing the cognitive routines that constitute a persons understanding of it" (p.194). He suggests that "a region will be defined as a set of interconnected entities..... conceived entities are interconnected when the cognitive events constituting their conception are coordinated as components of a higher level event" (p.198).

The noun schema has a feature that contains the morphemes that symbolize gender and number. In Danish those morphemes appear as affixes. Another feature contains purely semantic information about the primary domain of the region, and still another feature contains semantic information about the structure of interconnectedness. In our experimental computer model the possible values of purely semantic features are shown in figure 4 below:

NOUNS

1. DIMENSION
PROFILING IN A PRIMARY DOMAIN

FEATURE VALUE	DOMAIN
Physical	Space
TimeLoc	Time
Human	Human network
Nominal	Process
Proper	Situation

2. DIMENSION
STRUCTURE OF INTERCONNECTEDNESS

FEATURE VALUE	STRUCTURE
Part/Whole	Configuration of entities
Part	Part in configuration
Container	Inside/Outside
Path	Sequence
Abstract	Meaning by instantiation

Fig. 4

The semantic structure of adjectives, adverbs and prepositions are a-temporal relations as shown in figure 2. Prepositions are considered a prototype that symbolize spatial relation between two entities and it has no further characteristics. The adverb schema has a feature that contains purely semantic information concerning the nature of space. In our model the possible values are the following:

ADVERB

FEATURE VALUE	RELATION PROTOTYPE
Time	Relates a relation to time
Space	Relates a relation to space
Connect	Relates a relation to another linguistic structure
Intension	Relates a relation to degree of intension
Modal	Modality

Fig. 5

The adjective schema has a feature that contains the morphemes that symbolize degree.

5. Computer modelling

Parsing is a key concept of computer modelling of natural language understanding. In this context we think of parsing as the computational parallel to the term decoding (Langacker p.65-66) denoting the process of deriving knowledge structure from linguistic structure on the basis of a cognitive grammar.

In the preceeding paragraph it has been argued that a cognitive grammar is a lexical grammar in the sense that symbolic units in a lexicon function as building blocks of linguistic structure. Furthermore symbolic units function as processing units that interact with other units in order to compute a semantic representation. The processes not only interact with each other, but also with the human user in order to make decisions that cannot be made automatically. This concept differs fundamentally from the automatic and rule based concepts that can be derived from the generative paradigm. The experimental system that we are developing is outlined in figure 6 below.

PARSING ON BASIS OF A COGNITIVE GRAMMAR

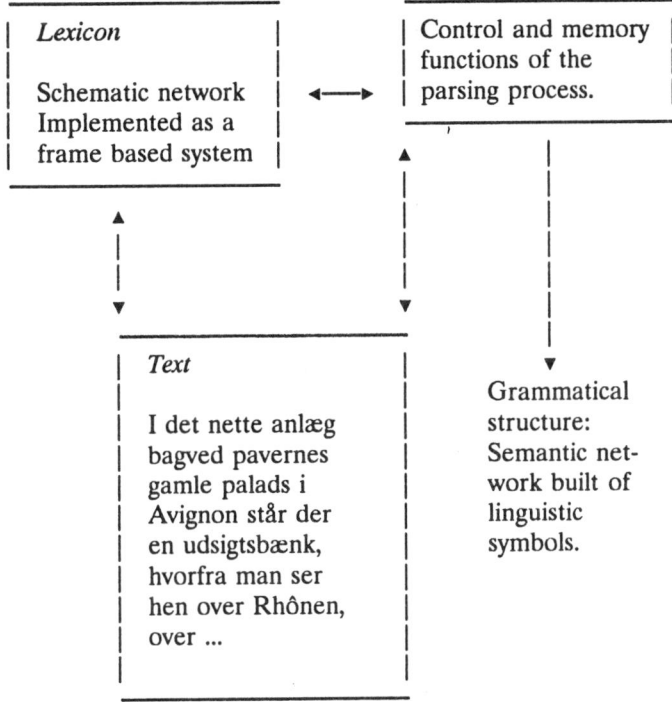

Fig. 6

The system is being developed in the Prolog language (Johns 1990). We have built a lexicon containing 4.000 Danish words according to the schemas that are described in the preceeding paragraph. On basis of the schemas the system recognizes all derived forms from their stem. The lexicon has been built by means of a software system that we have developed for the purpose. Concerning the feature values for purely semantic features we have made an experiment which shows that through an experimental learning process different people come to agree on the choice of feature values. It shows that the choice of features is solid.

Our parsing strategy is divided into two phases. During the first phase, which has been implemented, all words in the text are tagged with lexical information (Lytje 1990). During the second phase the semantic structures are computed. This phase has not been implemented yet, but as shown above, the algorithmic processes and the format of the resulting semantic structure have been thought out. Figure 7 below shows the three first sentences of the famous Danish short story *Fru Fønss* by I. P. Jakobsen, together with the semantic structure corresponding to the first sentence.

Fru Fønss
I det nette anlæg bagved pavernes gamle palads i Avignon står der en udsigtsbænk, hvorfra man ser hen over Rhônen, over Durances blomsterbed, over høje og marker og over en del af byen.

(In the pretty garden behind the popes' old palace in Avignon, there is a bench from which there is a fine view across the Rhône, beyond the Durance's flower beds, across hills and fields and a part of the town.)

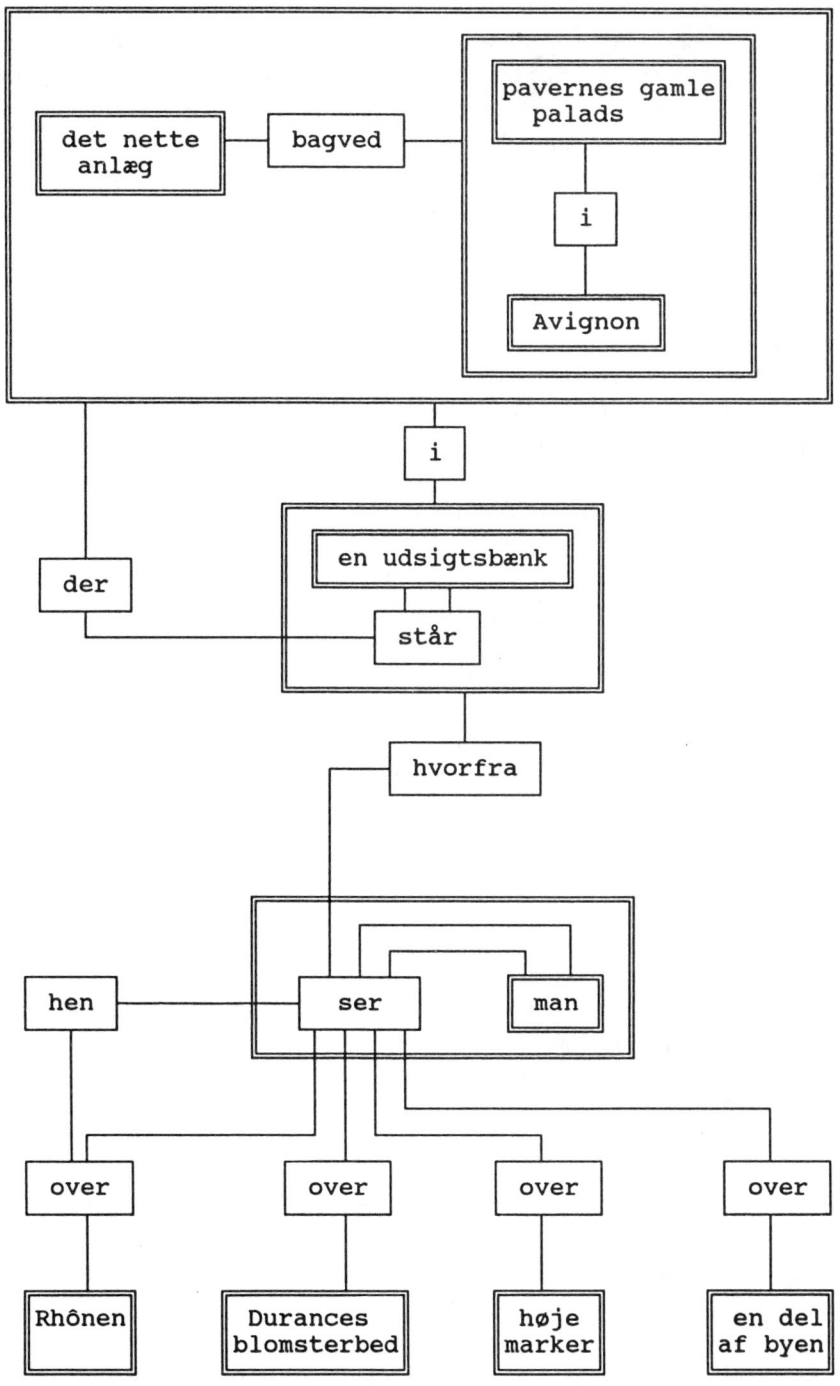

Fig. 7

6. Conclusion

Computer modelling can be seen as a research methodology for studying semantics: by implementing linguistic knowledge in a computer as a cognitive grammar our beliefs concerning semantics can be evaluated through practical use of the system. Semantic knowledge can be regarded as a kind of deep knowledge that may underly different applications such as systems for text analysis, language aquisition and knowledge aquisition.

The computer model we have suggested, and partly implemented, can be seen as a research tool for studying the relation between semantic structure and cognitive processes of understanding and comprehension. We have found that semantic structure can be computed by interacting algorithmic processes. The resulting structures are depicted as semantic networks representing nested trajector-landmark relations. These networks can be seen as a formal representation of the knowledge inherent in the text at a certain level of abstraction. And it can be seen as a computational model that may function as an inference structure for algorithmic processes that handle questions posed to the text.

Concerning computer modelling og natural language understanding we have suggested methodologies that seem to cope with some of the classical problems concerning ambiguity and undecidability. It is done by rejecting classical categories in favour of categorizing principles based on prototype and schematicity, that are implemented using frame based formulas. And it is done by rejecting a rule based parsing strategy in favour of interacting algorithmic processes, considering the human user one of the actors.

References

Allen, James (1987) *Natural Language Understanding*. Menlo Park, California: Benjamin/Cummings.

Hobbs, Jerry R. (1990) *Literature and Cognition*. Stanford, California: Center for the Study of Language and Information.

Johns, Nicky (1990) *MacProlog 3.0 Reference Manual*. London, England: Logic Programming Associates.

Lakoff, George (1987) *Women, Fire and Dangerous Things: What Categories Reveal about the Mind*. Chicago: University of Chicago Press.

Langacker, Ronald W. (1987) *Foundations of Cognitive Grammar*. Stanford, California: Stanford University Press.

Langacker, Ronald W. (1991) *Concept, Image and Symbol: The Cognitive Basis of Grammar*. New York: Mouton de Gruyter.

Lytje, I. (1990) 'Natural Language Understanding within a Cognitive Semantics Framework', in: *AI & Society* 4, 276-290.

Lytje, I. (1992) 'Formalisering som kognitionsvidenskabelig metode' (eng. "Computer modelling as a cognitive science methodology"). Unpublished. Denmark: Aalborg University, Department of Communication.

Lytje, I. (1992) 'Natural Language Understanding' in: *Encyclopedia of Microcomputers*. New York: Marcel Dekker.

Rich, Elaine (1983) *Artificial Intelligence*. Singapore: McGraw-Hill.

Schank, Roger & Abelson, Robert (1977) *Scripts, Plans, Goals and Understanding*. Hillsdale, New Jersey: Lawrence Erlbaum.

Schank, Roger (1980) 'Language and Memory', in: *Cognitive Science 4*, 243-284.

Vasey, Phil & Westwood, David (1990) *flex Expert System Toolkit*. London, England: Logic Programming Associates.

Winograd, Terry (1980) 'What does it mean to Understand Language', in: *Cognitive Science 4*, 209-241.

Winograd, Terry (1983) *Language as a Cognitive Process*. Menlo Park, California: Addison-Wesley.

Winograd, Terry (1986) *Understanding Computers and Cognition*. California: Addison-Wesley.

A Valency Based Description of Danish Verbs

Poul Søren Kjærsgaard and Lene Schøsler
University of Odense

0. Introduction

This article describes the application of valency theory in general and of the socalled Pronominal Method in particular to the description of Danish verbs.

The former will be described in section 1 of this article, and the latter in sections 2 through 4. In section 5, we shall briefly mention some areas where this approach is thought to be useful.

1. Fundamental assumptions

One of the basic assumptions is that any verb selects one or several dependents which may be valency bound or just placeholders. This assumption implies, in its turn, that the syntactic patterns surrounding verbs and other predicates may be adequately described by valency.

The selection of dependents basically involves the semantics of the verb, as it will hopefully appear from examples 1 through 3. Whether these dependents are actually present in the text or not, is another question which we shall not pursue here. May it suffice to say that the prevailing pattern seems to be syntactic optionality of the dependents.

The first step in our definition is to circumscribe the maximal number of possible valency bound dependents.
We do this by

1: using the test of negativity (by inserting negative pronouns)
2: substituting non-negative pronouns for the negative ones.

1.1 The negativity test

The test of negativity consists of exchanging a possibly valency bound dependent with a negative pronoun. If the presence of a negative pronoun prevents the action or the state described by the verb from taking place, the dependent is said to be valency bound. Examples:

1. Peter og Mary spiser spaghetti
   (Peter and Mary eat spaghetti)

2a. *Ingen* spiser spaghetti
    (Nobody eats spaghetti)

2b.   Peter og Mary spiser ingenting
        (Peter and Mary eat nothing)

In neither 2a nor 2b does the act of eating take place. *Peter og Mary* resp. *spaghetti* are accordingly defined as valency bound. It should be noticed, though, that the status of the two dependents is not identical. While *Peter og Marie* is obligatory, *spaghetti* is optional, compare:

3.   Peter og Marie spiser
        (Peter and Mary eat)

Danish uses at least five negative pronouns:

ingen [nobody], *ingenting/ikke noget* [nothing], *på intet tidspunkt* [at no time], *ingen steder* [nowhere], *ingenlunde/på ingen måde* [in no way]

Some of these pronouns may be ascribed primitive semantic features, thus allowing a rudimentary characterization of the dependent:

Ingen: + hum
Ingenting: − hum

1.2 Constraints on the negativity test

Some constraints apply to the use of the negativity test.

First of all, the sentence on which the substitution of a dependent takes place must be grammatically correct. Accordingly, the substitution is possible in 4a, but not in 4b:

4a.   Fiskeren ryger cigarer
        (The fisherman smokes cigars)

4b. * Vulkanen ryger ingenting
        (The volcano...)

Second, the choice of a negative pronoun is not arbitrary. It depends on the native speaker's competence.[1] And this competence is supposed to tell him or her that in 2a, the only possible negative pronoun is *ingen*.

It should be observed that the use of negative pronouns such as *ingen* and *intet* further allows a preliminary and rather coarse-grained semantic charac-

---

[1] The choice between *ingenting* and *ikke noget* appears to be governed by rather complicated rules.

terization of the dependents they replace: semantic features such as +*hum*, -*anim* apply to a dependent replaced by *ingen*.

Third, the test applies only on minimal phrases which include the verb, the subject and the complements to be tested (in the case of the subject being tested, the latter two coincide). If there were more complements, it would be impossible to determine the scope of the negation:

    5a.   Peter spiser ingenting om morgenen
           (Peter eats nothing in the morning)

In this sentence, one cannot determine whether the negation applies to the object of the act of eating or to the time the act of eating takes place.

Fourth, the negativity test can be applied on only one dependent at a time. If a sentence contains more than one negative pronoun, it becomes uninterpretable:

    6a.   *Ingen* spiser *ingenting*
           (Nobody eats nothing)

1.3 Problems with the negativity test

There is one problem related to the use of the negativity test. It can readily be shown that it overgenerates the number of possible valency bound dependents. On the basis of the following sentences:

    7a.   Peter spiser spagetthi om morgenen
           (Peter eats spaghetti in the morning)

    7b.   Peter spiser *på intet tidspunkt* spaghetti
           (Peter eats at no time spaghetti)

one might be tempted to conclude that because negation of the time indication prevents the action from taking place, *på intet tidspunkt* is a third valency bound dependent.

As probably any verb may combine with indications of time and place, it follows that considering such adverbials as valency bound becomes untenable if the notion of valency is to be useful. To distinguish indications of time or place from valency bound dependents (which may, of course, express time or place), some researchers have proposed the socalled *do so*-periphrasis[2], the Danish version of which is *gøre det*.

---

[2] cf. Lakoff and Ross (1977); Somers (1987).

The crucial thing about this periphrasis is that it replaces the verb+following valency bound dependents. Dependents which may be placed outside this periphrasis, are accordingly considered to be non-valency bound or adjuncts. In the case of 7a-b, this test would produce the following result:

7c.   Peter spiser spaghetti om morgenen, mens Henrik gør det om aftenen.
      (Peter eats spaghetti in the morning, while Henry does so in the evening)

The point is not that *gøre det/do so* might replace the verb and everything that follows it, including *in the morning*, but that *in the morning* **can** be placed outside the *do so*-perimeter. This possibility is accordingly interpreted as a sign that *in the morning* is peripheral (less important ≈ not valency bound) than the dependent which could not possibly be placed outside the perimeter, i.e. *spaghetti*.

In case indications of time and space are valency bound (after verbs such as *vare* (take), *bo* (live) they would fall inside the boundary:

8a.   Filmen varede en time, men det gjorde teaterstykket ikke
      (The film took one hour, but the play didn't)

8b.   Peter bor i Odense, men det gør Marie ikke
      (Peter lives in Odense, but Mary doesn't)

1.4 Insertion of pronouns
After having defined the number of valency bound dependents and a preliminary semantic characterization of these dependents, we can proceed to a syntactic characterization of the valency bound dependents by inserting positive pronouns. To the extent that these pronouns have case markers, this will allow to distinguish functions such as subject and object.

The results obtained so far will be transferred to a description of the socalled proportionality relation, which among other things will allow us to distinguish different readings of the verb, as will be shown in sections 2 through 4.

2. The pronominal approach applied to Danish
2.1 Basic assumptions of the pronominal approach
The basis of the pronominal approach (PA) is the observation that a permanent relationship, which we call *a relation of proportionality,* holds between the valency bound NPs on the one hand and the corresponding pronouns on the other. Thus we observe a constant relation between the

personal pronoun *hun* (she) and the various lexicalizations of the grammatical subject in the following three examples:

9. Hanne ryger en stor cigar
   (Hanne is smoking a big cigar)

10. Fiskerkonen ryger en laks
    (the fisherman's wife is smoking a salmon)

11. Hvem af kvinderne ryger hvad?
    (which of the women is smoking what?)

There is also a relation of proportionality between the personal pronoun *den/det* (it) and the lexicalizations of the grammatical object of the three examples.

The aptitude of the pronouns to substitute NPs and thus to clarify their syntactic functions is well known to Danish romanists, as the traditional university grammars make use of a pronominal test of substitution in order to identify valency bound NPs. But it is important to distinguish the pronominal substitution test from the PA. The most important difference between the pronominal substitution test and the PA is the directionality of the relationship: in a traditional substitution test, the NPs are considered the basic forms, whereas the PA considers the pronominal forms basic in the sense that they indicate the syntactic and semantic valency schemes of the verb by means of their paradigmatic inventory. The lexicalized forms, which do not present such inflected forms of valency relevance, are considered by PA as expansions of the pronominal forms.

Thus, the PA takes its methodological starting point in the paradigmatic inventory of the pronouns, which can be labelled the "function" words of language itself. It is therefore an immanent method, as opposed to other methods that depart from language external definitions of valency.

It is possible to derive a language-immanent, and non-ontological semantic system based on the primitives: +/-animate, +/-human, +/-neutral from the pronominal paradigm. It may turn out to be useful to add more semantic distinctions, such as +/-concrete, +/-specific, but for the time being we restrict the semantic features to these three.

2.2 The application of the PA to the Danish verb *ryge* (smoke)

We claim that the PA offers a language-immanent, complete and coherent description of the valency of Danish verbs, as it has already proved to be capable of describing French and Dutch verbs. A result of the valency description of the verbs is the identification of different readings of the verbs.

The verb *ryge* (smoke) can serve as an illustration. Let us consider three more examples of the verb *ryge*:

12. Hanne ryger
    (Hanne smokes)

13. vulkanen ryger
    (the volcano smokes)

14. skamlen ryger hen ad gulvet
    (the stool slides across the floor)

If we want to describe the verb *ryge* from the six examples quoted, we have to deal with at least two important problems that deserve further discussion in subsections:
A: The first problem concerns the number of implicit or explicit valency bound forms (2.2.1);
B: The second problem concerns the different pronominal paradigms (2.2.2).

2.2.1 The number of valency bound forms

Let us first consider the number and type of the valency bound forms. The examples 9-11 and 14 are bivalent: the verb selects its subject, its direct object 9-11 or locative object 14. The exemples 12 and 13 have just one valency bound form, i.e. the subject. The question is whether the direct object is optional and implicit in the examples 12, 13 and 14 or whether we have to deal with different valency schemes? If we consider 12, a direct object is in fact implicit as a NP such as *en stor cigar* (a big cigar) can reasonably be inserted. In 13 and 14 there is no possible insertion of an NP, which is proved from the impossibility of a passive transformation of these cases.

The number and type of valency bound forms suggest the distinction of three different readings of the verb *ryge* i.e.: a monovalent RYGE_1, exemplified in 13, a bivalent (subject/object) RYGE_2, exemplified in 9-12 and a bivalent (subject/locative object), exemplified in 14.

2.2.2 The pronominal paradigms

In this section, we shall discuss the pronominal paradigms of the subject and of the object.

The subjects of the first four examples differ from that of the fifth, as the first four subjects are proportional to *hun* (she), and the subject of 13 is proportional to *den* (it). In basic semantic terms this means that the subject of the examples 9-12 has the semantic features +animate, +human, whereas that of 13 has the semantic features -animate, -neutral (perhaps also

+concrete). In 14, the subject can be both *hun* and *den*, i.e. the semantic features +/-animate, +/-human, -neutral.

Thus, the different pronominal paradigms of the subjects support the distinction made in 2.2.1 in RYGE_1, RYGE_2 and RYGE_3.

Let us consider the pronominal paradigms of the objects of RYGE_2. In the examples 9-11 all objects are proportional to *den* (it), corresponding to the semantic features -animate, -neutral (perhaps also +concrete). Thus, the paradigm does not suggest a further reading distinction of RYGE_2. However, if we take into account the degree of cohesion between the verb and its object, we observe a difference suggesting a distinction between 9 and 12 on the one hand and 10 on the other. In the first case (examples 9 and 12), it is only possible to have a very special type of implicit object, i.e. a cigar, a pipe, tobacco, etc. In the second case (example 10), it is not possible to understand an object such as cheese, salmon, etc. Such an object must be explicit[3], in order to obtain the meaning of the verb seen in 10. The tendency of the object to be present or - on the contrary - to be freely understood, urges us to subdivide RYGE_2 into two readings: RYGE_2, with an optional object, as exemplified in 9 and 12 and RYGE_4, with an obligatory object, as exemplified in 10. As for the example 11, this is a genuine ambiguity.

In the case of RYGE_3, illustrated by 14, the locative object is obligatory. A construction as 14a:

14a. skamlen ryger
     (the stool smokes)

can only be interpreted as an instance of RYGE_1, like 13, and not as a case of 14, without explicit locative object.

The discussions in the sections 2.2.1 and 2.2.2 lead to the following schematic description of the Danish verb RYGE:

---

[3] It is evident that almost any term, normally considered as "obligatory", can be understood in an appropriate context. But that is not relevant here. The meaning of the term obligatory - as opposed to optional - is that in "neutral" speech, without any special stress or contrastive effect, the obligatory term will be present.

RYGE_1

SUBJECT

-animate
-neutral
{hvad for én/et,
 hvad, den/det}

ex.13: vulkanen ryger
no passive transformation

RYGE_2

SUBJECT	[OBJECT]
+animate	-animate
+human	-neutral
{hvem, jeg,	{hvad for én/et,
vi, man}	hvad, den/det}

exx. 9, 12: Hanne ryger [en stor cigar]
+ passive transformation

RYGE_3

SUBJECT	LOCATIVE
+/-animate	
+/-human	
-neutral	
{hvem,jeg,vi,man	{hvorhen}
hvad for én/et,	
hvad, den/det}	

ex.:14: skamlen ryger hen ad gulvet
no passive transformation

RYGE_4

SUBJECT	OBJECT
+animate	-animate
+human	-neutral
{hvem, jeg, vi, man}	{hvad for én/et, hvad, den/det}

ex. 10: Hanne ryger en stor laks
+ passive transformation

NB: optionality is indicated by means of square brackets [ ]. The pronominal paradigm is given between curly brackets { }.

2.3 Conclusion of section 2.2
The study of the verb *ryge* (smoke) has shown the ability of the PA to define the valency of a verb, in the sense that it characterises - morphologically and semantically - the type of valency bound forms of a verb. Concerning the number of valency bound forms and their degree of cohesion to the verb, the PA does not offer a particular test battery, it simply makes use of the well-known methods mentioned in section 1. It should be stressed, however, that the PA focuses on the distribution of the pronominal paradigms of the valency bound forms. This explains why this immanent method is less exposed to the dangers of subjectivity and consistency that are so disastrous for valency projects. We think that the immanent nature of the PA makes it a solid starting point for a computerized valency description.

In this very short presentation of the PA applied to Danish there is only time to discuss the most essential aspects of the method. A discussion of a more complicated case than the verb *ryge*, i.e. the verb *flytte* (move), in the following section, gives us the opportunity to go into more detail, in particular to discuss the number of valency bound forms and the types of pronominal paradigms.

3. Application of the PA to the Danish verb *flytte* (move)
We will base our description of the verb *flytte* (move) on the following seven examples:

15.   Vinden flytter sand fra vestkysten til østkysten
      (the wind transports sand from the West coast to the East coast)

16.   Hanne flytter tasken over i vindueskarmen
      (Hanne removes her bag to the window sill)

17. Elefanten flytter den ene fod
(the elephant moves one foot)

18. Hanne flytter fra Odense til Århus
(Hanne moves from Odense to Århus)

19. Hanne flytter
(Hanne moves)

20. Hanne flytter fra Peter
(Hanne moves out on Peter)

21. De flytter fra hinanden
(They move apart)

As we did in the case of *ryge*, section 2.2, we will first consider the number of valency bound forms in section 3.1, then the types of pronominal paradigms in section 3.2.

3.1 The valency bound forms of the verb *flytte* (move)

The verb *flytte* is construed with **one** valency bound form: the subject, cf. example 19; with **two**: the subject and the object, cf. example 17; and with several PPs indicating direction that may be considered valency bound forms, cf. the examples 15, 16 and 18. With the exception of examples 20 and 21 to be dealt with below and in section 3.2, these PPs may be considered lexicalizations of one or two locative objects, indicating the direction to or from a place, proportional to *hvorfra* (from ...where) and *hvortil* (where... to). If we apply the *do so*-test mentioned in section 1, we find that these PPs are in fact valency bound:

18a. Hanne flytter fra Odense og det gør Peter også /... *fra Århus
(Hanne moves from Odense and so does Peter / ... *from Århus

18b. Hanne flytter til Århus og det gør Peter også /... *til Odense
(Hanne moves to Århus and so does Peter / ... *to Odense)

The locative objects are optional, whereas the objects are obligatory. These differences urge us to make a distinction between FLYTTE_1 with four valency bound forms: the subject, the object and two locative objects, as illustrated by the examples 15-17 and FLYTTE_2 with three valency bound forms: the subject and two optional locative objects in examples 18-19. This distinction is supported by the fact that only FLYTTE_1 permits a passive transformation. The following 15a passive transformation of 15 is correct:

15a. Sandet flyttes/bliver flyttet af vinden fra vestkysten til østkysten
(the sand is moved/tranported by the wind from the West coast to the East coast)

unlike 18a which is not a correct passive transformation of 18 and of FLYTTE_2; 18a can only be interpreted as a passive transformation of 18b, involving FLYTTE_1:

18a. Hanne flyttes fra Odense til Århus
(Hanne is moved/transferred from Odense to Århus)

18b. nogen flytter Hanne fra Odense til Århus
(somebody moves/transfers Hanne from Odense to Århus)

In the examples 20 and 21 there are only two valency bound forms, i.e. the subject and a PP, the nature of which is to be discussed in 3.2. The PP cannot be considered a locative object like the ones we have seen in the case of FLYTTE_2. Thus, we will distinguish between three readings of *flytte*: FLYTTE_1, FLYTTE_2 and FLYTTE_3.

3.2 The pronominal paradigms of *flytte* (move)

Let us consider the pronominal paradigms of the three readings, first that of the subjects.

The subjects of FLYTTE_2 and FLYTTE_3 are proportional to {hvem, jeg, vi, man} i.e. the semantic features +animate, +human. The subjects of FLYTTE_1 are proportional to {hvem, jeg, vi, man, hvad for én/et, den/det, hvad} i.e. the semantic features: +/-animate, +/-human, -neutral. Thus, the pronominal paradigms of the subjects support the distinction between FLYTTE_1 on the one hand and FLYTTE_2 and FLYTTE_3 on the other but they do not suggest further subdivisions.

The object of FLYTTE_1 is proportional to the paradigm {hvem, dig, os, hinanden, hvad for én/et, den/det, hvad} i.e. the semantic features: +/-animate, +/-human, -neutral.

The locative objects of FLYTTE_1 and FLYTTE_2 are both proportional to the proforms[4]: *hvorfra* (from where?) and *hvortil* (where to?). The second valency bound form of FLYTTE_3 is by no means proportional to *hvorfra* or *hvortil*; it is to be considered a prepositional object introduced by 'fra' (from) followed by an NP proportional to the paradigm {hvem, dig, os}, i.e. the semantic features +animate, +human. Thus, the study of the pronominal

---

[4] cf. Gebruers (1991) for a discussion of the most appropriate terminology for the PA, in particular the discussion of the terms *pronoun* and *proform*.

paradigms of the valency bound forms suggests the following schematic presentation of the verb *flytte*.

FLYTTE_1

SUBJECT	OBJECT	[LOC]	[LOC]
+/-animate +/-human -neutral {hvem, jeg, vi, man} {hvad for én/et den/det} {hvad}	+/-animate +/-human -neutral {hvem, dig, os, hinanden} {hvad for én/et, den/det} {hvad}	{hvorfra}	{hvortil}

ex.: 15,16,17: vinden flytter sand fra vestkysten til østkysten
+ passive transformation

FLYTTE_2

SUBJECT	[LOC]	[LOC]
+/-animate +/-human -neutral {hvem, jeg, vi, man} {hvad for én/et den/det} {hvad}	{hvorfra}	{hvortil}

ex.: 18-19: Hanne flytter fra Odense til Århus
no passive transformation

FLYTTE_3

SUBJECT	PREPOSITIONAL OBJECT: *FRA* + NP
+animate	+animate
+human	+human
{hvem, jeg,	{hvem, dig,
vi, man}	os, hinanden}

ex.: 20-21 De flytter fra hinanden
no passive transformation

4. Comparison with traditional descriptions of Danish verbs

In section 2.3 we asserted that the immanent nature of the PA makes it a better starting point for a valency description than the traditional methods. Let us prove this assertion by resuming the traditional presentations of the two verbs studied here, as they are found in *Ordbog over det danske sprog* (ODS) and *Dansk sprogbrug* (DS).

4.1 Traditional description of *ryge*

Both ODS and DS distinguish the readings of *ryge* on purely semantic criteria, although these are not explicitly stated. These criteria induce ODS to distinguish six readings of the verb, whereas DS only distinguishes three. This implies that there is a partial overlap between the readings of the two studies. This clearly illustrates the lack of general agreement of analyses based on non-explicit, intuitive semantic criteria - even in a rather simple case like *ryge*.

ODS distinguishes the following six readings that are followed by a quotation:

A. afgive, udsende røg [emit, give off smoke, smoke]:
   hele Sinai Bjerg røg
   (the whole of Mount Sinai smoked)

B. udsende småpartikler [emit small particles], afgive synlige dampe [give off visible fumes]:
   Hugleiks blod ryger endnu
   (Hugleik's blood is still steaming)

C. frembringe røg [produce smoke]:
   ryge .. med Virack og Myrre
   (smoke...with incense)
   ryge tobak
   (smoke tobacco)

>   ryges som en hollandsk sild
>   (to be smoked like a kipper)

D. ufrivillig, hurtig bevægelse [unvoluntary quick movement]:
   en skammel .. røg hen ad gulvet
   (a stool slid across the floor)

E. formålsbestemt hurtig eller pludselig bevægelse [intentional quick movement]:
   haren røg ud af busken
   (the hare shot out from the bush)

F. forstærkende betydning:
   Herrens vrede skal da ryge imod denne mand
   (the wrath of the Lord is going to strike this man)

DS distinguishes the following three readings that are followed by a quotation:

A. kakkelovnen/vulkanen ryger
   (the stove/the volcano smokes)
   ryge en laks, ryge en ræv ud af hulen
   (to smoke a salmon, to smoke a fox out of its hole)

B. han ryger cerutter/på en pibe/som en skorsten
   (he smokes cigars/a pipe/like a chimney)

C. chancen røg, flasken røg på gulvet
   (his chances went up in smoke; the bottle fell on the floor)

It is worth noticing that the readings A and B of DS correspond to reading C in ODS.

4.2 Traditional description of *flytte*

In the case of *flytte*, ODS bases the reading distinction not on semantic, but on syntactic criteria, although they are not explicit. The criteria adopted by DS are neither explicit nor comprehensible:

ODS distinguishes (A) a transitive and (B) an intransitive reading:

A. bringe/føre noget fra et sted til et andet [to bring sth. from one place to another]

B. skifte bopæl/opholdssted/tjeneste/plads [to change residence/job]

DS distinguishes two readings:

A.　　flytte et møbel/en patient [move a chair or a patient]
　　　flytte om på møblerne [move the furniture around]

B.　　flytte ind/fra byen/fra hinanden/hjem/sammen med ... [move in/out of town/away from each other/home/together with]

4.3 Evaluation of the traditional descriptions

In the traditional descriptions it is striking that the basic criteria for establishing reading distinctions are implicit and apparently random: in the case of *ryge*, the criteria are clearly semantic, in the case of *flytte*, they are syntactic - at least in ODS. We observe the lack of consistency, not only in the basic criteria of one and the same dictionary (ODS: *ryge* - *flytte*), but also lack of consistency between ODS and DS when they apply the same, i. e. semantic, criteria (*ryge*). These observations emphasize the need for elaborating clear and language immanent criteria that make intercoder consistency possible.

5. The Pronominal Approach Applied to Lexicon-Based Parsing

The ultimate goal of our work is to describe the Danish verbs from a valency based viewpoint. Besides our theoretically based work, we have started to investigate some areas where a valency based approach seems to be a versatile tool. We shall briefly indicate two such areas.

Most teachers of foreign languages (even closely related ones) have experienced how often students make mistakes in verb construction. Whether consciously or not, they apply constructions of their mother tongue or another foreign language on the language in question. An easily accessible bilingual database seems to be a possible way of decreasing the error rate.

Valency based descriptions also seem to be useful in the case of natural language processing, partly for the sake of obtaining intercoder consistency, partly in the case of lexicon-based parsing. The crux of this approach is to make use of the predictions about the environment which can be inferred from the presence of frame-bearing words (verbs, nouns, adjectives). A valency database is thought to form a good starting point for such an approach.[5]

Up to this point, we have used a testbed version, implemented in HyperCard©. This version is a convenient tool for the coding of new verbs and for editing existing entries. It also contains a useful interface to Prolog.

---

[5] cf. Starosta/Namura: Lexicase (1986); McCord (1980); cf. also Swedish work on a lexicon parser as reported in M. Toporowska Gronostaj (1990).

The work reported in this paper was made possible due to a gift from the Danish Research Council for the Humanities. The HyperCard© testbed was implemented by Bradley Music.

References

Blanche-Benveniste, Claire, Deulofeu, José, Stefanini, Jean, van den Eynde, Karel (1987) *Pronom et syntaxe. L'approche pronominale et son application au français*, deuxième édition augmentée, Paris.

Bruun, Erik (1980) *Dansk Sprogbrug* (DS), 2nd edition, Copenhagen.

Gebruers, Rudi (1991) *On Valency and Transfer-Based Machine Translation*, Leuven.

Lakoff, G. and Ross, J. R. (1976) 'Why You Can't Do So Into the Sink'; in: McCawley, J.D. (ed) *Syntax and semantics*, vol. 7.

McCord, M. C. (1980) 'Slot Grammars'; in: *American Journal of Computational Linguistics* 6,1. pp. 41-53.

Ordbog over det danske sprog (ODS) (1918-1955) edited by H. Juul-Jensen et alii, Copenhagen.

Somers, H. (1987) *Valency and Case in Computational Linguistics*. Edinburgh.

Toporowska Gronostaj, M. (1990) *Om LPS verbvalenslexikon. En artbetsrapport från projektet: En Lexikonorienterad Parser för Svenska* (LPS). Institutionen för språkvetenskaplig databehandling. Göteborgs Universitet.

Cognitive Models as Discourse Representation

Ole Ravnholt
University of Roskilde

Introduction

A discourse is usually taken to be a piece of connected and meaningful text or speech, a unified whole of language use, rather than just a collection or sequence of sentences, connected only by contiguity. A discourse may be written or spoken by one or more discourse participants, depending on what kind of discourse it is: books, lectures, conversations, exchanges of letters and postcards can all be regarded as examples of (kinds of) discourses.

Two principal factors appear to make discourse out of sequences of sentences (Johnson-Laird 1983, 395):

1. *connectedness* in the form of referential coherence between sentences as evidenced by the resolution of anaphoric reference and ellipsis in discourse understanding (among other things); and
2. *plausibility* with respect to world knowledge common to the discourse participants, whether in the form of commonly assumed general background knowledge or of knowledge communicated or assumed in the ongoing discourse.

The theoretical approaches to discourse comprehension which serve as a starting point for the following discussion are Johnson-Lairds (1983) mental models theory as it is applied to discourse by Johnson-Laird himself and by Alan Garnham and his colleagues (e.g. Garnham 1987, Garnham & Oakhill 1985, Garnham, Oakhill & Vonk 1989), and AI-oriented work by Barbara Grosz, Candace Sidner and many others, comprehensively reviewed and compiled in Grosz & Sidner (1986) and in Grosz, Pollack & Sidner (1989). One important thing they have in common is the claim that representation of content (discourse referents with their properties and mutual relations) is the important part of discourse representation, i.e. what is represented is not just (or, in the case of Garnham: not) linguistic expressions.

Finally, I will propose an investigation of the possible merits of a cognitive semantics approach to discourse representation. Evidence for theories of this kind can be obtained in many ways and from many sources. So far, I have been especially interested in the types of relationships between anaphors and their antecedents and in memory for discourse.

Types of Anaphora
1. Cospecification by identity or lexical generalisation

    a small office ..   *the office/ it*
                                   the room

2. Specification by association, inference, or computation

    a circus ...   *the artists/ they*
                                  the trapeze artist
    the dead heiress ...   *the murderer*
    a meeting ...   *the third meeting*

3. Specification of an element or subset of a set

    a herd of elephants...   *the elephant/ the elephants/ those/ the one(s) in front*

With 'vague quantifiers' this can be quite intriguing:

    Few MPs were present at the meeting.
    They felt the issue was important ...
        (the subset of MPs actually referenced)
    They had gone for a beer ...
        (the complement of the subset of MPs actually referenced)

4. Reference to the generic concept

    There were only few camels by the river. *They* go a long way without water.

Memory for Discourse
1. Coreferential descriptions are confused more often than non-coreferential ones:

    The man with the martini is tall.
    The man standing by the window is tall.

2. Implicit instruments and agents are confused with highly probable ones, but neither of these with improbable ones.

John opened the lock (with a key/hooked nail).
They were surprised to find that the rubbish had not been collected (by the dustmen/army).

3. Prepositional phrases with different meanings are confused if they are used in sentences which probably describe the same situation, but not otherwise:

The hostess bought a mink coat from the furrier/ in the furrier's.
The hostess received a telegram from the furrier/ in the furrier's.

4. General terms (nouns and verbs) are remembered differently depending on the context in which they occur:

The food was left uncovered. The insects buzzed around it.
In the garden was a hive. The insects buzzed around it.
The housewife cooked the chips. The housewife cooked the peas.

5. Specification of generic terms takes time: Subjects take longer to read a sentence with an instance noun if it follows a sentence in which that noun's referent was only described as a member of a more general category, but only when the first sentence does not suggest what kind of instance the category-member is.

$$\left\{\begin{array}{l}\text{The weapon}\\ \text{The knife}\end{array}\right\} \left\{\begin{array}{l}\text{was protruding from the corpse.}\\ \text{was found beside the corpse.}\\ \text{had been effective.}\end{array}\right\}$$

Mental Models

The starting point of Philip Johnson-Laird's theory of mental models (1983) is that human beings do not appear to make inferences by formal, logical rules, but rather by an ability to construct and manipulate mental models from which conclusions can be read directly. This ability is also claimed to be applied in discourse comprehension. This aspect of mental models theory has been worked out in Garnham 1987 (orig. 1981) and in later work by Garnham and his colleagues.

Two claims are important in the mental models approach to discourse. In Garnham's (1987) (somewhat dogmatic, in my view, but therefore illuminating) wording they are

1. 'texts and discourse are encoded in mental models, and (...) these representations are the psychologically important ones.' (Garnham 1987, 19)

2. '... representations of discourse should centre around tokens standing for things that the discourse is about, rather than for expressions in it.' (Garnham 1987, 20)

ABC of Reasoning with Mental Models

Reasoning, according to Johnson-Laird (1983), is accomplished in a three step procedure:

1. construct a mental model of the first premise;
2. add the information in the further premises to the model, looking for counterexamples and adding more models as needed;
3. find the relation between the 'end' terms that holds in all those models.

For example, if the first premise is *Some of the Artists are Beekeepers*, the model will be like 1. below, representing a situation in which there are some artists and some beekeepers, at least some of which are identical, while others may not be. It is important to keep in mind that the elements of the model are abstract tokens to which arbitrary roles can be assigned, not words, as it were.

Then, when the information from the second premise: *All the Beekeepers are Chemists* is added and integrated we get model 2. so that the logical conclusion: *Some of the Artists are Chemists* can be read from the model, rather than deduced from the premises. There may of course also be artists that are neither beekeepers nor chemists as well as chemists that are neither artists nor beekeepers.

1. *Some of the Artists are Beekeepers*

   artist = beekeeper
   artist = beekeeper
   (artist)(beekeeper)

2. *Some of the Artists are Beekeepers*
   All the Beekeepers are Chemists

   artist = beekeeper = chemist
   artist = beekeeper = chemist
   (artist)(beekeeper)= chemist
   (chemist)

What is not clear is the effect of background knowledge in this context: in what ways does it influence the construction of models. What would happen, e.g., if the As, Bs and Cs were related to each other independently of the discourse in an abstraction hierarchy (as might be the case in everyday reasoning which is concerned with things related in many different ways to each other in the real world, rather than abstract tokens with arbitrary relations). If the As in the example above had been trees and the Bs birches (so that *Some of the Trees are Birches*), you would still need As that are not Bs, but not the other way round, since birches are a kind of tree (model 3. below).

If the Cs were cedars, the second premise (*All the Birches are Cedars*) would probably be discarded as false (and therefore not integrated in the model) by any sane and knowledgeable practical reasoner, since birches and cedars are different kinds of trees, so that even though one can build models like 4., of which it is true that *Some of the Trees are Cedars* and which could be a model of the real world, it does not reflect the premises.

3. *Some of the Trees are Birches*   4. *Some of the Trees are Birches*
                                           Some of the Trees are Cedars
    arbor = betula   arbor = betula
    arbor = betula   arbor = betula
    (arbor)   arbor = cedrus
                                           arbor = cedrus
                                           (arbor)

A model that integrates the premises in the same way as for artists, beekeepers, and chemists, and of which the conclusion *Some of the Trees are Cedars* would of course be true, could not also be a model of the real world:

5. *Some of the Trees are Birches*
    All the Birches are Cedars
    arbor = betula   = cedrus
    arbor = betula   = cedrus
    (arbor) (betula) = (cedrus)
                       (cedrus)

From a logical point of view, of course, the empirical truth or falsity of premises (or conclusions) does not affect the validity of arguments. But if, as it has been shown, practical reasoning is influenced by knowledge about the world, then the assumed empirical status of premises (and of conclusions, by the way: if a valid argument leads to a preposterous conclusion, you attack the premises) must influence the construc-tion of the mental models applied.

Other similar difficulties involve other kinds of real-world relatedness as they are reflected e.g. the anaphoric relationships mentioned. One example is part-whole relationships, like the following example (from King 1986) in which the defini-teness of the NP of the second sentence cannot straightforwardly be accounted for by mental models theory (nor, I think, by any simple hypotheses about discourse structure):

A circus was in town last week. *The trapeze artist* was phenomenal.

One can plausibly claim that a circus could be part of an instantiated mental model after the first sentence, but hardly that all of its component parts would also be there. Actually, since trapeze artists are not necessary, but only highly probable, components of a circus, one can not know that there is a trapeze artist in this particular circus without being told. The mention of *circus* in the first sentence creates a context in which it is very likely that a trapeze artist is singled out sufficiently to be eligible for definite reference, but probably not an instantiated mental representation of a trapeze artist. If such a representation is created it should be accomplished by the definite NP of the second sentence, in which the artist is mentioned for the first time, rather than by the first sentence which only sets the stage.

The problem here is that mental models are such 'meagre' representations, e.g. in the sense that they do not appear to have defaults or implicit potentialities. Possibly this is a consequence of the demand that they must be 'instantiated', at least if that means fully explicit.

Even if such considerations could be discarded for syllogistic reasoning, they would still hold for discourse comprehension, since plausibility with respect to background world knowledge is claimed to be an important factor in this.

Models and Propositional Representations

The form of mental models 'is distinct from that of propositional representations. A model *represents* the state of affairs and accordingly its structure is not arbitrary like that of a propositional representation, but plays a direct representational or analogic role. Its structure mirrors the relevant aspects of the corresponding state of affairs in the world.' (Johnson-Laird 1981, 174). However, to ensure that the consistency of the mental model constructed can be checked, not only with respect to the preceding version of the model and the latest premise (in propositional form), but with respect to all the premises involved, a double representation of discourse is taken to be necessary, with propositional representations ('close to surface linguistic structure') as well as mental models, but used for different purposes. The relationship between the two is described as a mapping of 'propositional representations into mental models of real or imaginary worlds: *propositional representations are interpreted with respect to mental models.*' (Johnson-Laird 1983, 156).

However, since the mechanism applied in discourse comprehension is supposed to 'consist of a device that constructs a *single* mental model [whereas in syllogistic reasoning up to three models must be constructed, to reach the correct conclusion, or] on the basis of the discourse, its context, and background knowledge' (Johnson-Laird 1983, 128), the model constructed is like the configuration of the pieces on the chess board in that it does not incorporate a representation of its own history, of how it came about. For chess this is a feature, not a bug, but for inferencing and discourse comprehension it is a problem.

Mental Models in Discourse Comprehension

Plausibility has to do with the content of the discourse and its relation to the (physical, social, etc) world in that it 'depends on the possibility of interpreting the discourse in an appropriate temporal, spatial, causal, and intentional framework' (Johnson-Laird 1983, 371), i.e. it depends on the possibility of constructing a single mental model that is consistent not only internally, but also with the history of the discourse (i.e. with a propositional representation of previous input sentences, as for inferencing) and with background knowledge about the domain it concerns. Discourses that violate basic assumptions, beliefs or expectations are experienced as abnormal.

Speakers maintain referential coherence by adhering to the Gricean principle of being helpful to their listeners: they try to restrict the possible interpretations of their discourse to a single one. If this restriction is not successful, the listener will usually ask for clarification - i.e. he will request from the speaker that he must choose between possible interpretations - or he will have to bear the extra burden of keeping track of several models until the discourse progresses to let him integrate them into a single one.

One (if not the most) important aspect of referential coherence is the resolution of anaphoric expressions (such as pronouns, definite descriptions, nominal and verbal ellipses and sub-stitutions). Again, this poses problems for mental models theory, because, even though a mental model should contain a representation of all the candidate antecedent referents for an anaphor, this is not sufficient for its resolution.

One problem is that the linguistic structure of the discourse together with global focusing and local centering mechanisms (see below) impose preference orderings of the candidate antecedents that differentiate and restrict their eligibility at any given point in the discourse. The history of a discourse must contain more than a chronological sequence of propositional renderings of the sentences it comprises. Focusing is a property of the discourse as such, not of its individual sentences.

Another problem is that pronouns match only antecedents of their own gender. For English mental models this a minor problem since English has only 'natural gender' (sex, that is) which is a property of the referent, not its linguistic ex-pression. However, many other languages (including most of the European ones) have grammatical gender, which is a property of expressions, not of referents: male is not necessarily masculine (or vice versa), even though it may cause some confusion when natural and grammatical gender are in conflict. If, in German, where the pronouns determined by natural gender (*er, sie*) are also used to match grammatical gender, a discourse referent has been introduced as *das Mädchen*, she may subsequently be referred to as *es*, matching the grammatical gender of the expression, but also as *sie*, matching her natural gender. If she had been introduced more personally as *Elke*, however, she would probably always be *sie*. In Danish, where natural gender pronouns (*han, hun*) are distinct from grammatical gender pronouns (*den, det*), natural gender overrides grammatical gender if it is prominent: *pigen* (the girl) is subsequent-ly *hun*, not *den*; *barnet* (the child) however, may be *det* or *han/-hun*. Even though propositional representations are supposed to be 'close to surface linguistic form', they do not seem to be sufficient to account for phenomena of this kind. Even Alan Garnham, who used to do his best to purge every trace of linguistic expression from mental models has become worried by it, having apparently visited the continent.

Problems with Mental Models as Discourse Representations

It would appear that the two central claims - that the psychologically important representations of discourse are mental models, and that they should centre around tokens standing for things that the discourse is about, rather than for expressions in it - do not hold, at least not in the strict interpretation advocated by Garnham and, as far as I can see, also by Johnson-Laird, even though his focus on inferencing, rather than discourse, makes it less plain. In the current formulation of the theory, propositional representations are as important psychologically as mental models, since they are necessary to get the rest to work, and even though referents must certainly be represented mentally, so must at least some aspects of the linguistic expressions involved.

To sum up, the main problems with mental models theory as a theory of discourse representation are:

1. two different, permanent (or at least: long term) representations of the entire discourse are posited to get the theory to account for the empirical findings that sometimes content appears to be retained in memory, and sometimes linguistic expressions;
2. mental models have too little structure, and the relationship between the structures manifested in mental models and those found in background knowledge is too weak to account for the establishment of discourse referents that may be referred to anaphorically;
3. mental models do not properly account for the history and structure of the discourse, nor for the focusing and centering - structures that appear to be accessed in the resolution of anaphora, nor for the linguistic and intentional structures (see below).

AI Models

The theory proposed by Grosz & Sidner (1986) is a theory of discourse structure, not of the nature of mental representations. Therefore information or knowledge structures are suggested that can be taken as prerequisites for human (and machine) discourse comprehension, rather than formats for the representation or implementation of such structures in the mind. The structure of a discourse is viewed as a composite of three distinct, but interacting components[1]:

1. a linguistic structure, i.e. the 'grammatical' structure of the actual sequence of utterances in the discourse in terms of segmentation and of coordination and subordination of segments;
2. an intentional structure, the basic elements of which are discourse intentions and the relationships between them, primarily dominance (goal/subgoal relationships) and satisfaction precedence (temporal ordering of goals);
3. an attentional state with information about the objects, properties, relations and discourse intentions that are most salient at any given point.

Linguistic Structure - Segmentation
Utterances are aggregated into discourse segments, the boundaries of which may be explicitly marked by linguistic expressions: certain words or phrases or more subtle cues, such as intonation or changes in tense and aspect. Such boundary markers provide information at the discourse level, not the sentence level: they indicate changes in the intentional or attentional structures. Boundaries may also be indicated implicitly by the relationships between utterance-level intentions and active discourse segment purposes.

In its turn, discourse segmentation affects the interpretation of linguistic expressions, e.g. it constrains the use of anaphoric referring expressions such as pronouns or definite NPs.

---

[1] These components will be exemplified in the following on a couple of small pieces of text taken from the beginning of Hans Christian Andersen's fairy tale *Fyrtøjet*. No pretention with respect to the possibilities of extending these considerations to literary analysis is made. An English gloss of the text can be found in the appendix.

```
⎡DS1        1.   "Kan du see det store Træ?" sagde Hexen og pegede
│                paa det Træ, der stod ved siden af dem.
│           2.   "Det er ganske huult inden i!
│           3.   Der skal Du krybe op i Toppen,
│           4.   saa seer Du et Hul, som Du kan lade Dig glide igjen-
│                nem og komme dybt i Træet!
│           5.   Jeg skal binde Dig en Strikke om Livet, for at jeg kan
│                heise Dig op igjen, naar du raaber paa mig!"
│ ⎡DS2      6.   "Hvad skal jeg saa nede i Træet?" spurgte Soldaten.
│ │         7.   "Hente Penge!" sagde Hexen, "Du skal vide ...
│ │                 ...
│ │         8.   ... tag Du af Kisten saa meget Guld, Du vil!"
│ │         9.   "Det var ikke saa galt!" sagde Soldaten.
│ │
│ │ ⎡DS3   10.   "Men hvad skal jeg give Dig, din gamle Hex? For noget
│ │ │            vil Du vel have med, kan jeg tænke!"
│ │ │      11.   "Nei," sagde Hexen, "ikke en eneste Skilling vil jeg
│ │ │            have!
│ │ │      12.   Du skal bare tage til mig et gammelt Fyrtøi, som min
│ ∟ ∟            Bedstemoder glemte, da hun sidst var dernede.
│ ⎡DS4     13.   "Naa! lad mig faa Strikken om Livet!" sagde Soldaten.
∟ ∟
```

Intentional Structure

Discourses are plan-based: they have purposes; for any discourse, one such purpose, the *discourse purpose*, will provide its foundation, whereas the *discourse segment purposes* specify the contribution of discourse segments to the overall discourse purpose. It is characteristic of discourse or discourse segment purposes that they are intended by speakers to be recognized; in fact, it is essential to their achieving the intended effect that they are recognized by listeners. The motivation to participate in a discourse is distinct from the discourse purpose and external to the discourse itself. The motivation for any participant to engage in a discourse may be private, not intended to be recognized: a speaker who engages in a discourse with the aim of impressing some other participant(s) will probably have a better chance of succeeding if that motivation is not recognized, but the discourse employed for it will not be understood if the discourse purpose is not recognized (it may of course be quite impressive anyway, but that's a different story).

The satisfaction of the discourse purpose is a main purpose of the discourse, whereas the satisfaction of discourse segment purposes *contributes* to the satisfaction of their *dominating* discourse or discourse segment purpose. Dominance relationships are linked by equivalence rules to *support* relationships between propositions, and *generate* relationships between actions.

Furthermore, the temporal order in which purposes are satisfied may be significant, i.e. discourse segment purposes may have a *satisfaction-precedence* relationship with each other. So, even though there is no finite list of possible discourse purposes, the number of possible relations between purposes is quite small. The intentions in the above piece of text and their dominance/satisfaction-precedence relations are given below:

I1:	(Intend W_{itch}(Intend S_{oldier} (Go S into-tree)))	I1 dom I2
I2:	(Intend S (Intend W (Tell W S why)))	I1 dom I4
I3:	(Intend S (Intend W (Tell W S why)))	I2 dom I3
I4:	(Intend S (Tell S W (Intend S (Go S into-tree))))	I2 sp I4

Attentional Structure

The global attentional state is modelled by a *focusing structure* consisting of a stack of *focus spaces*, each associated with a discourse segment, which contain the entities (objects, properties, and relations) that are salient at that point in the discourse, including the discourse segment purpose. A new space is pushed onto the stack whenever the discourse segment purpose for a new segment contributes to that of a preceding segment. If the space for that segment is not on top of the stack, the spaces above it are popped from the stack. The attentional state model constrains the range of discourse segment purposes that are considered as candidates for domination or satisfaction-precedence of the current discourse segment purpose, and the search for possible referents of definite NPs and pronouns. Within each focus space, candidates are ordered according to local focusing mechanisms, involving preferences based on syntactic as well as semantic criteria (Sidner 1983). The attentional structure of the text is shown below.

The intentional structure provides a complete history of the discourse purposes established so far and the relations between them, whereas the focusing (or attentional) structure is related only to the current state of the discourse, or rather, to currently unresolved purposes, but with a built-in structuring of its elements that depends on the linguistic structures and expressions that provided its basis. At the end of a discourse, then, there will be a fully developed intentional structure, whereas the focus stack will be empty.

```
                                    | tinderbox₁₂ |
                                    |    I3       |
                                    |    FS3      |
                                    └─────────────┘
                  | gold₈       |   | gold₈       |
                  |  ...        |   |  ...        |
                  | money₇      |   | money₇      |   | string₅ |
                  |  I2         |   |  I2         |   |  I4     |
                  |  FS2        |   |  FS2        |   |  FS4    |
                  └─────────────┘   └─────────────┘   └─────────┘
| string₅ |       | string₅     |   | string₅     |   | string₅ |
| tree₁   |       | tree₁       |   | tree₁       |   | tree₁   |
|  I1     |       |  I1         |   |  I1         |   |  I1     |
|  FS1    |       |  FS1        |   |  FS1        |   |  FS1    |
└─────────┘       └─────────────┘   └─────────────┘   └─────────┘
```

Cognitive semantics

To conclude, I would like to propose an investigation of the possibility of using cognitive models (here given as frames) of the sort proposed by Lakoff (1987) to replace the mental models of Johnson-Laird and Garnham. They have far more structure in them because they are built from abstract cognitive schemas rather than just tokens. The information used in building the representation of the discourse will then come partly from utterances in the discourse itself and partly from more permanent cognitive structures of semantic and background world knowledge. The beginning of the fairy tale might then look something like the following:

Der kom en Soldat marcherende henad Landeveien: een, to! een, to!

> **schema:** path
>   **departure:** <place>
>   **destination:** <place>
>   **path:** the road
>   **direction:** towards dest.

> **schema:** soldier
>   **abstr:** human
>   **sex:** default: male
>   **gear:** defaults:...
>   **body parts:** defaults:..
>   **movement:** march
>   .....

```
schema: human
    sex:        {female, male}
    age:        {integer, young, old, ...}
    body parts: defaults: back, side, chest, lower lip,..
    movement:   {walk, run, ..., march, ...}
    ......
```

The road is represented by an instantiation of the path schema described by Lakoff, with the slots for the departure and destination left open. The soldier schema is a specialization of a more general schema for humans which is not instantiated directly, but from which it inherits some of its properties while others are local (or 'soldier specific').

han havde sit Tornister paa Ryggen og en Sabel ved Siden, for han havde været i Krigen, og nu skulde han hjem.

```
schema: path                        schema: soldier
    departure: the war                  abstr: human
    destination: home                   sex: male
    path: the road                      gear:   pack (pos: back)
    direction: homeward                         sword (pos: side)
                                                defaults: ...
                                        body parts: back, side, defaults:..
                                        movement: march
                                        .....
```

Probably, the definiteness of expressions in the second sentence for referents that have not been mentioned before can be accounted for in terms of expectations set up by the open or default slots already in the representation. If one can find ways of representing local focusing in these structures as well (and I think the format will prove sufficient for that) they can replace the focus spaces in Grosz and Sidner's attentional state, thus giving the beginnings of a representation with the richness required to account for the linguistic and memory structures that can be found in discourse.

Appendix
Text 1
1. "Do you see that big tree?" said the witch and pointed at the tree that stood beside them.
2. "It is quite hollow inside!
3. You must climb to the top,
4. there you will see a hole that you can slip through and get deep into the tree!

5. I will tie a string around your body, so that I can haul you out again when you call me!"
6. "What am I to do inside the tree?" asked the soldier.
7. "Fetch money!" said the witch, "You must know ...

   ...
8. ... take from the chest as much gold as you want!"
9. "That doesn't sound so bad!" said the soldier.
10. "But what do I give you, you old witch? Because you'll want something, I can imagine!"
11. "No," said the witch, "I do not want a single penny!
12. You just take for me an old tinderbox my grandmother forgot when she was last down there!"
13. "Well! Get the string around me!" said the soldier.

Text 2
There came a soldier marching along the road: one, two! one, two! he had a pack on his back and a sword by his side, for he had been to the war and was now going home.

References
Garnham, Alan (1987a). *Mental Models as Representations of Discourse and Text*. Chichester: Ellis Horwood.
Grosz, Barbara & Candace L. Sidner (1986): 'Attention, Intentions, and the Structure of Discourse', in: *Computational Linguistics*, 12.3.
Grosz, Barbara, Martha E. Pollack, & Candace L. Sidner (1990): 'Discourse', in: M.I. Posner (ed): *Foundations of Cognitive Science*, Cambridge, Mass.: MIT Press.
Johnson-Laird, P.N. (1983): *Mental Models*, Cambridge: CUP.
Lakoff, George (1987): *Women, Fire, and Dangerous Things*, Chicago, University of Chicago Press.
Oakhill, J.V. & A. Garnham (1985). 'Referential Continuity, Transitivity, and the Retention of Spatial Descriptions', in: *Language and Cognitive Processes* 1.149-162.
Oakhill, J.V., A. Garnham & W. Vonk (1989). 'The on-line construction of discourse models', in: *Language and Cognitive Processes* 4: 263-86.
Sidner, Candace L. (1983): 'Focusing in the Comprehension of Definite Anaphora', in: Michael Brady & Robert C. Berwick (eds): *Computational Models of Discourse*. Cambridge, Mass.: MIT Press.

Frozen expressions in Danish and French

Susanne Nøhr Pedersen
Center for Language Technology

1. Introduction
Machine translation of more or less idiomatic expressions poses a series of problems and challenges. Some machine translation systems do not have any strategy for treating such expressions and thus indirectly accept a wrong translation. Other machine translation systems have made attempts to list such expressions in the dictionary. But as such a list will be extremely long and probably never exhaustive, a third strategy for at least a subset of more or less idiomatic expressions is under consideration in Eurotra, the EEC machine translation project.

Since the middle of 1991, Eurotra groups in Denmark, France, Greece and Italy have worked on a contrastive analysis of constructions of the type 'N0 + be + Prep1 + N1 (+ Prep2 + N2)'. As the investigations are far from being finished, only preliminary results can be presented in this paper.

In the formula in question, N0 is either a noun phrase, an infinitive clause or a *that*-clause. The verb 'to be' (*være*) - which is rather empty of meaning and whose function is reduced to being a carrier of mood, tense and aspect - is followed by a preposition that again is followed by a noun phrase (N1). 'Prep2 plus N2' might be filled or empty. If filled, N2 is either a noun phrase, an infinitive clause or a *that*-clause.

However, this formula covers many subgroups. Focus in this article will be on the so called 'frozen expressions', as in e.g.:

(1)   N0   +   be   + Prep1   + N1   +   (Prep2 + N2)
        Projektet   er   på   forkant   med udviklingen
        (The project is at the forefront of development)

In section 2. the corpus of the investigation is presented. In 3., a definition as well as observations on Danish frozen expressions are made. In 4., some preliminary contrastive observations with respect to structural similarities and differences between French and Danish will be made. In 5., representational issues are considered. And finally in 6., some final remarks are given.

Normally, the Danish examples have been translated into English. Translations are given in parenthesis, i.e. ( ). Sometimes a literal translation will be given, either because it has been difficult to find a precise translation or to illustrate a specific point. Literal translations are marked by square brackets [..].

Steen Jansen et al (eds): Computational Approaches to Text Understanding,
© Museum Tusculanum Press, Copenhagen 1992

2.0 Corpus

A corpus can be composed in many different ways and these will lead to different results. Consequently, the point of departure must be a description of the kind of results that are aimed at.

In the present study the aim is to identify some specific constructions that are actually used in the kind of texts (i.e. technical texts), Eurotra is working on. Moreover, one basic criterion for setting up the corpus has been that the text must originally have been written in Danish, i.e. not translated.

The actual text corpus has been composed by 1) two Eurotra texts on telecommunications (17.225 words), 2) a biotechnological corpus (1 mill. words) and 3) the DANwORD corpus (1.250 mill. words) which has only been partially examined. The corpora are machine readable, but not tagged.

The biotechnological corpus (bioda) has been searched in full by means of an automatic search programme, developed by Henrik Holmboe and his assistants (The Aarhus School of Business). Eurotra-DK has set up the search patterns as well as several filters that proved necessary to avoid too many irrelevant examples.

As the linguist's 'Sprachgefühl' is likely to become distorted after long periods of immersion in a problem, introspection has only been used to a very small extent. I.e. it has been used when there are several readings of an expression, but only one reading has been identified by means of the corpus.

Thus a total of 92 different expressions have been identified.

3. Observations on Danish
3.0 Definition

By a frozen expression we will understand an expression in which the number and kind of constituents in the sequence 'Prep1 (..) N1' are fixed. Fixed in the sense that no constituent within the sequence 'Prep1 N1' can be omitted or added without distorting the meaning of the expression as such:

(2) Et nyt forslag er i støbeskeen.
 (A new proposal is in the melting-pot)

* Et nyt forslag er i den gode støbeske.
* (A new proposal is in the good melting-pot)

* Et nyt forslag er på støbeskeen.
* (A new proposal is at the melting-pot)

Besides the syntactic definition above, a semantic criterion may be useful in order to identify frozen expressions: generally, these expressions do not have a compositional meaning. This means that the meaning of the whole expression cannot be derived from the meaning of the single constituents.

As stated in section 1., frozen expressions belong to a subgroup. However, this subgroup can be divided into still more subgroups. In the list below, which is not considered complete, the most important ones are mentioned.

'Prep2 N2' is not possible (33 examples):
(2')   Et nyt forslag er i støbeskeen.
       (A new proposal is in the melting-pot)

   *   Et nyt forslag er i støbeskeen for udviklingen.
   *   (A new proposal is in the melting-pot for the development)

Note that (2') might be followed by an adverbial phrase, prepositional or not; if prepositional it is not considered as part of the construction. 'Prep2 N2' is always valency bound by the lexical head of 'Prep1 N1'.

'Prep2 N2' is obligatory (24 examples):
(3)   Forskerne er på forkant med udviklingen.
       (The researchers are at the forefront of development)

   *   Forskerne er på forkant.
   *   (The researchers are at the forefront)

'Prep2 N2' is optional (21 examples):
(4)   For tiden er han ikke i ligevægt.
       (For the moment he is not in equilibrium)

       For tiden er han ikke i ligevægt med sig selv.
       (For the moment he is not in equilibrium with himself)

Obligatory adjective - no variation possible (6 examples):
(5)   Forskerne er på den sikre side.
       (The researchers are on the safe side)

   *   Forskerne er på siden.
   *   [The researchers are on the side]

   *   Forskerne er på den dårlige side.
   *   [The researchers are on the bad side]

Obligatory adjective - variation possible (6 examples):
(6)   Forskerne er på god/dårlig/venskabelig fod med hinanden.
       (The researchers are on good/bad/friendly terms with one another.)

* Forskerne er på fod med hinanden.
* (The researchers are on terms with one another)

Obligatory presence of possessive determiner (2 examples):
(7)   ... vil det måske være på sin plads med lidt baggrundsinformation om: Selve satellitterne.
[... will it maybe be on its place(=appropriate) with some background information about: The satellites themselves]

* ... vil det måske være på plads med lidt baggrundsinformation om: Selve satellitterne.
* [... will it maybe be on place with some background information about: The satellites themselves]

Thus, in (2), (3) and (4) no adjectival modification of N1 is acceptable. The difference between (2) and (3) is that (2) does not allow the 'Prep2 + N2' to be filled whereas (3) requires it to be filled. In (4) 'Prep2 + N2' may or may not be filled. In both (5) and (6) an adjectival modification of N1 is required. The difference between (5) and (6) is that in (5) the lexical realization of the adjective is fixed whereas (6) allows for more than one lexical realization of the adjective. But still in (6) an adjective must be present. In (7) the presence of a possessive determiner modifying N1 is required.

To sum up, in what follows the constructions in (2)-(7) will be called frozen constructions, as they are defined by the fixedness of all constituents in 'Prep1 (Det/pos.pron) (Adj) N1'.

3.1.0 Properties

Having given a definition of frozen expressions, we shall have a look at some of the basic properties and distributional characteristics shared by such constructions.

3.1.1 The function of *være* (be)

One basic property in this type of construction is that 'to be' is a support verb, i.e. a verb rather empty of meaning whose function is reduced to being a carrier of e.g. mood, tense and aspect. Thus the semantic core of the construction is not contained in the verb itself, but is contained in 'Prep1 N1 (Prep2 N2)'.

This observation can be substantiated by the fact that in cases where 'Prep2 N2' is filled, 'Prep1 N1' is the frame bearing element, and not the verb 'to be'. Hence, what is argued is that the predicate in such constructions is not a form of *være* (be), but 'Prep1 N1 (Prep2 N2)'.

3.1.2 Pronominalization

In expressions belonging to the subtypes in question, 'Prep1 + N1 (+ Prep2 + N2)' can be pronominalized by means of *det* (so), just like 'be + adj':

(8)   De japanske satellitter er på forkant med udviklingen - og det er de amerikanske også.
(The Japanese satellites are at the forefront of development and so are the American ones)

which shows that 'Prep1 + N1 (+ Prep2 + N2)' is one constituent.

However, the same goes for locatives (cf.9a below). But in contrast to e.g. the example in (8), locatives can also be pronominalized by means of *der* (there) as in (9b) or *der* (there)+*preposition* as in (9c):

(9)   a. Peter er i spisestuen - og det er Marie også.
[Peter is in the dining-room and that is Marie also]

   b. Peter er i spisestuen - og der er Marie også.
[Peter is in the dining-room and there is Marie also]

   c. Peter er i spisestuen - og Marie er også derinde.
[Peter is in the dining-room and Marie is also in there]

In Danish the pronoun *det* is the unmarked (less restrictive) form - it just fills the syntactic function. Whereas *der* is the marked form (more restrictive) that apart from assigning a syntactic function also marks 'place' and 'space'. Also adverbs made up by *der+preposition* (e.g. *derinde, derimellem, deri*) can take this function. These adverbs compared to *der* emphasise the place/space meaning of the sentence. In the following, nothing but cases and readings of cases that can only be replaced by *det* will be discussed. The cases and readings of cases that can be replaced by *det* as well as *der* or *der+prep* will not be considered.

3.1.3 Modification

Just like subject complements formed by adjectives, frozen expressions allow for modification usually by means of adverbs of degree:

(10) a. De japanske satellitter er helt nye.
(The Japanese satellites are totally new)

   b. De japanske satellitter er helt på forkant med udviklingen.
(The Japanese satellites are totally at the forefront of development)

3.1.4 Coordination of Prep1 + N1 (+Prep2 + N2) and an adjective

Quite often 'Prep1 + N1 (+Prep2 N2)' constructions allow for coordination with an adjective:

(11)   De japanske satellitter er billige og på forkant med udviklingen.
       (The Japanese satellites are inexpensive and at the forefront of development.)

This permits us to assign a more precise syntactic function to 'Prep1 + N1 (+Prep2 N2)', namely that of subject complement.

However, examples are found in which coordination with an adjective is very doubtful, if not ungrammatical, as in e.g.:

(12) * Forskerne er entusiastiske og på den sikre side.
     * (The researchers are enthusiastic and on the safe side.)

What is illustrated in (12) is rather a question of semantic restrictions than of syntax.

3.1.5 Aspectual variants

Quite often aspectual variants of the support verb *være* or its synonym *befinde sig* (= neutral aspect) are observed, i.e. inchoative, durative, terminative or causative variants.

(13) a. Neutral aspect:
        Patienten er/befinder sig i koma.
        (The patient is in a coma)

   b. Inchoative aspect:
      Patienten går/kommer i koma.
      (The patient goes into a coma)

   c. Durative aspect:
      Patienten ligger i koma.
      (The patient will remain in a coma the next few weeks)

   d. Terminative aspect:
      Patienten kommer ud af koma om et par uger.
      (The patient will get out of coma within a few weeks)

   e. Causative aspect:
      Medicinen bringer patienten ud af koma.
      (The medicine will bring the patient out of coma)

In practice, a given 'Prep1 N1 (Prep2 N2)' will rarely allow for all aspectual variants. The most frequent aspectual variants are inchoative and causative.

The properties described in sections 3.1.1. - 3.1.6. above should not to be considered in isolation. Note that most of the properties are also shared by constructions in which the support verb is followed by a noun phrase, as in *Peter har ansvaret for rapporten* (Peter has the responsibility for the report). For a more detailed description of this type of Danish constructions, the reader is kindly referred to Nøhr Pedersen (1989).

4.0 Contrastive observations

It is a well known fact that there is far from always a structurally one-to-one mapping between frozen expressions in one language and frozen expressions in another language. Investigations based on about 100 examples in French and Italian reveal that the percentage of similar constructions in these two Romance languages is about 65 %, whereas the figure for French and Danish is about 50 %. Precise figures will not be given as the input list received from France was not transparent in all respect.

Focus in section 4 will be on differences and similarities between French (source language) and Danish (target language) and on how frozen expressions should be rendered if a one-to-one mapping does not exist.

4.1 Structural similarity

Several examples are found in which a one-to-one mapping is feasible from French to Danish, as in e.g.:

(14) Cette entreprise est au bord de la faillite.
 =>
 Denne virksomhed er på fallittens rand.
 (This company is on the brink of bankruptcy.)

However, although the structures in French and Danish are similar, the verb *être* must sometimes be translated into a verb that differs from *være* (be):

(15) Son salaire est en proportion de son poste.
 =>
 Hans løn står i forhold til hans stilling.
 [His wages stand in proportion with his post.]

(16) Cette rue est dans le prolongement de l'autre.
 =>
 Denne gade ligger i forlængelse af den anden.
 [This street lies in continuation of the other.]

The verbs *stå* (stand) og *ligge* (lie) have the same function as *være* (cf. 3.1.0.) and are thus considered 'support verbs'.

In other cases there is free alternation in Danish between a form of *være* (be) and a form of *stå* (stand):

(17) a. Le pilote est en liaison avec sa base.
 =>
 b. Piloten står i forbindelse med sin base.
 [The pilot stands in contact with his base.]

 c. Piloten er i forbindelse med sin base.
 [The pilot is in contact with his base.]

Examples also exist in which the alternation does not seem totally free:

(18) ... les journalistes sont aux écoutes .....
 =>
 ... journalisterne er/står/ligger   på lur ....
 [... the journalists are/stand/lie   on the watch....]

If in Danish you *er* (are) på *lur* (on the watch), a complement introduced by *efter* (after/for) is required. Whereas if you *står* (stand) or *ligger* (lie) *på lur* (on the watch) a complement is less likely to appear.

4.2 Structural similarity or structural dissimilarity

In two cases a fairly free choice exists between a translation into a similar structure and a translation into a dissimilar structure.

The first case we will consider is where a choice exists between a similar construction and a construction in which the French 'Prep1 N1' is translated into a Danish ordinary verb. This is true if a corresponding verb exists, as in e.g.:

(19) a. L'avion est en feu.
 =>
 b. Flyet er i brand.
 [The plane is in fire.]

 c. Flyet brænder.
 [The plane burns.]

The choice between the two translations will of course depend on the context, but in many cases it will just be a matter of taste. However, it can be argued that b) expresses a static meaning whereas c) expresses a more dynamic meaning (durative).

The second case we shall consider is where a choice exists between a similar construction and a construction in which the French 'Prep1 N1' is translated into a Danish adjective and the French adjective modifying N1 is translated into a Danish adverb. This is true if a corresponding adjective exists, as in e.g.:

(20) a. Ce travail est de la première urgence.
=>
b. Dette arbejde er af yderste vigtighed.
(This work is of the utmost importance)
c. Dette arbejde er yderst vigtigt.
(This work is very important)

Some regularity has been observed with respect to this translation pattern in so far as Prep1 in French is likely to be *de* and an adjective is likely to be obligatorily present in the French frozen expression, i.e. * *Ce travail est d'urgence.*

The choice between the two translations into Danish can be considered a matter of stylistics.

4.3. Structural dissimilarity

The structural dissimilarities observed as a result of a translation into Danish can be summarized by means of the following main groups among which (21) and (22) are the most frequent:

(21) 'être + Prép1 N1' => 'verb'
La Commission est dans l'attente d'une réponse.
=>
Kommissionen afventer/venter på et svar.
(The Commission awaits/waits for an answer)

(22) 'être + Prép1 N1' => 'be + adjective'
Ce livre est d'actualité.
=>
Denne bog er aktuel.
(This book is of current interest)

Other translation cases as illustrated in (23) - (27) can also be observed:

(23)   'être + Prép1 N1' => 'support verb + NP'
       La France est en froid avec la Chine.
       =>
       Frankrig har et køligt forhold til Kina.
       [France has a cool relationship towards China]

(24)   'être + Prép1 N1' => 'verb + adverb'
       Ce tableau n'est pas d'équerre.
       =>
       Dette maleri hænger ikke lige.
       (This painting is not straight)

(25)   'être + Prép1 N1' => 'verb + particle'
       Il est en faveur de ce projet.
       =>
       Han er for dette projekt.
       (He is for the project)

(26)   'être + Prép1 N1' => 'paraphrase'
       Le projet est en question.
       =>
       Der stilles spørgsmålstegn ved projektet.
       (The project is called in question)

To sum up, the different translation cases illustrated in sections 4.1 - 4.3 above show that there are no means of predicting how a frozen expression will be translated into the target language. Therefore, elaborating a representation which allows for the maximum use of lexical transfer rules will be of crucial interest.

5. Representational issues

In this section representational issues are discussed. This topic has recently been subject to an investigation in Eurotra. What follows draws heavily upon the outcome of this investigation.

The Eurotra Interface Structure (IS) level in its present shape is an elaboration of dependency systems (cf. Hays 1964, Hudson 1984, Mel'čuk 1979 and, in Machine Translation, Vauquois 1975) in that every phrase is made up of a governor optionally followed by dependants of two types: arguments and modifiers. Arguments are elements which are bound to the governor or head of each construction whereas modifiers (adjuncts or circumstantials in other terminologies) are less tightly bound by the governor.

In contrast to other dependency models, the Eurotra model is characterized by its lowered governor approach, i.e. the predicative core has its valency bound elements as sister nodes.

An informal IS representation of a sentence like *Les chercheurs sont à genoux devant le ministre* is illustrated below (fr_lu = French lexical unit):

(27)   Les chercheurs sont à genoux devant le ministre

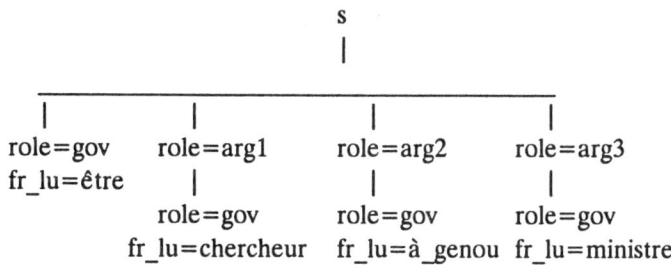

The IS representation in (27) is problematic in so far as there is not only 'one' possible translation into Danish of *être*. Seen in isolation, it is difficult to defend a dictionary entry saying: *être* => *ligge*. Moreover, as stated in 3.1.1, the type of construction being studied in this paper is characterized by the fact that the predicate is not *être*, but 'Prep1 N1'. This finding is not reflected in the structure of (27).

One solution to this problem is to delete the support verb, store the information about which support verb the actual 'Prep1 N1' is constructed with in the monolingual dictionaries and allow 'Prep1 N1' to be the governor of the whole sentence, as in (28):

(28)   Les chercheurs sont tout à fait à genoux devant le ministre.

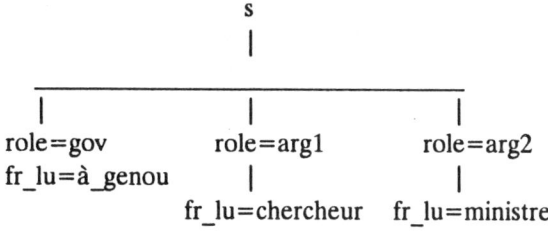

However, this solution faces a number of difficulties since, in particular, with respect to modifying elements we must be able to distinguish in the structure between say sentence adverbs and adverbs modifying the governor *à genou*. As Eurotra's current specifications forbid branching governors, yet another solution has been considered.

This solution consists in having a dummy sentential governor as informally illustrated in the representation given below:

(29)   Malheureusement, les chercheurs sont tout à fait à genoux devant le ministre.

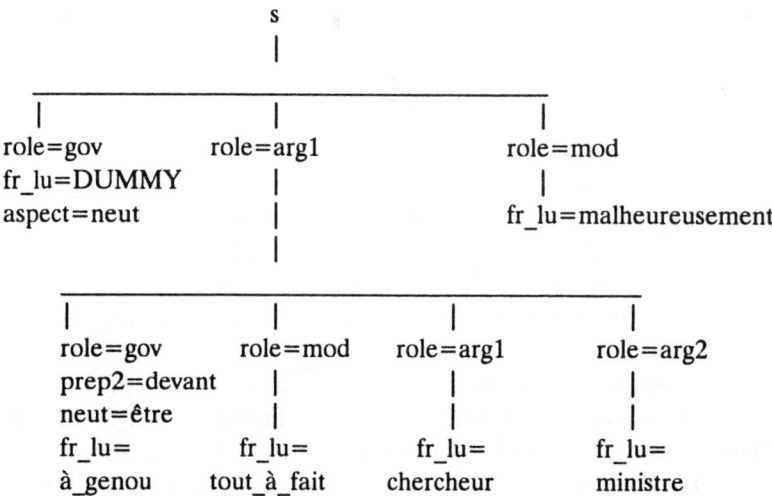

Thus, what is translated by default is a dummy lexical value whose instantiation depends on 'Prep1 N1', which is interpreted as the semantic head of the sentence. In contrast to (28), (29) allows us to distinguish different types of modifying elements, i.e. sentence modifiers are represented as sisters to the dummy node and non-sentence modifiers are represented as sisters to 'prepN'(= *à_genou*).

At IS level in the synthesis module, *på_knæ* is looked up in the Danish monolingual lexicon where the entry contains information about which support verb(s) *på_knæ* can be constructed with. The Danish IS representation is illustrated in (30) where 'da_lu' means Danish lexical unit:

(30)   Desværre ligger forskerne helt på knæ for ministeren.

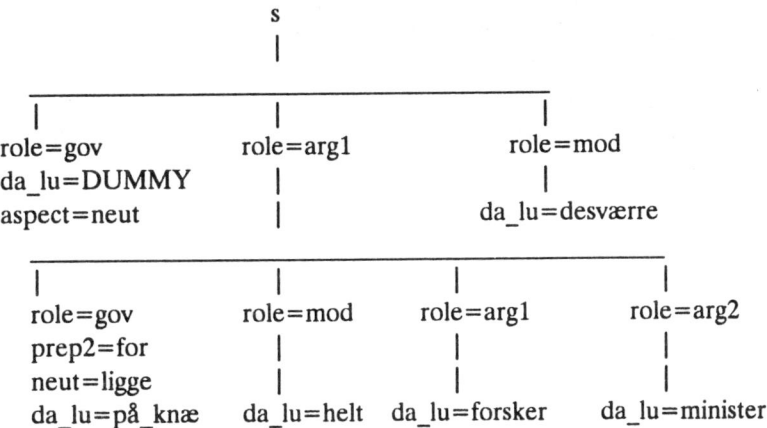

Finally between IS synthesis and ERS (Eurotra Relational Structure) an insertion of the Danish support verb as governor of the sentence takes place.

6. Final remarks

In the introduction to this paper, attention was drawn to the fact that in other machine translation systems which claim to be able to handle frozen expressions, the solution consisted in listing such expressions, i.e. *être à genoux* => *ligge på knæ*. Considered in isolation, this solution might at first seem attractive. But given that the verb can be conjugated and furthermore can allow for modification, different aspectual variants as well as negation, this solution presupposes that the lexicographer is able to make an exhaustive list of occurrences. This would be a very time consuming, if not impossible job. Furthermore, such a list will just be a listing of problematic cases, and not a theoretically founded solution to the problem.

Seen in a broader perspective, contrastive investigations of this kind can hopefully not only be useful in connection with machine translation, but also in connection with the elaboration of bilingual dictionaries for human translators.

References

Danlos, L. (1988) 'Les expression figées', in: *Langages*, 90, pp. 23-37.
Hays, D. (1964) 'Dependency theory: a formalism and some observations', in: *Language*, 40, pp. 511-525.
Hudson, R. (1984) *Word Grammar*. Blackwell: Oxford.
Mel'čuk, I.A. (1979) *Dependency Syntax: Theory and Practice*. New York: SUNY.

Nøhr Pedersen, S. (1989) 'The Treatment of Support Verbs and Predicative Nouns in Danish', in: *Papers from the Seventh Scandinavian Conference of Computational Linguistics*, pp. 208-217. Reykjavik 1990.

Nøhr Pedersen, S. & Kirchmeier-Andersen (1989) 'Contrastive Linguistics in Eurotra', in: *Papers from the CL-symposium at The Aarhus School of Business,* pp. 155-186, Aarhus 1991.

Vauquois, B. (1975) *La traduction automatique à Grenoble*. Paris: Dunod.

Negation in Eurotra: An attempt at determining the scope of negation for NPs functioning as subject, object or prepositional object.

Bjarne Ørsnes
Center for Language Technology

1. Preface

The present paper presents the strategy for determining the scope of negation developed in the machine translation project EUROTRA. Characteristic for this treatment is that it mainly deals with negation from a linguistic point of view and that it has been implemented in a running machine translation system.

The strategy is considered to be 'euroversal' (i.e. applicable to all official EC-languages) and one of the goals of the present paper is to discuss its general applicability to Danish.

This paper draws heavily on the chapter of negation in the EUROTRA reference manual (1990), written by Heleen Hoekstra, Utrecht.

2. Standard negation

The kind of negation treated here is commonly referred to as 'standard negation'. Standard negation is defined as:

> 'that type of negation that can apply to the most minimal and basic sentences' (Payne 1985, p. 198)

Payne in turn defines 'basic sentences' as sentences consisting of a single predicate with as few noun phrases and adverbial modifiers as possible (Payne, 1985, p. 198). In order to identify standard negation a set of tests has been established, originating from the treatment of negation in English by Klima (1964). The two most important are:

1. Standard negation permits 'either'-conjoining.

   (1)   It is*n't* raining, and it is*n't* snowing, *either*

2. Standard negation permits positive, rather than negative tag questions.

   (2)   It does*n't* rain, *does it*?

   (3)   It rains, *doesn't it*?

Even though these tests were developed originally for English, they seem to hold for Danish as well. The second test, however, is especially useful in Danish as we have two different particles for the formulation of tag-questions. In case of standard negation we use the particle *vel*:

(4)   Det regner *ikke, vel*?
        (It doesn't rain, does it?)

And in all other cases we use the particle *ikke* (which by the way is identical to the negation element):

(5)   Det regner, *ikke*?
        (It rains, doesn't it?)

By means of this 'tag'-test it is possible to distinguish standard from non-standard negation. Cf.

(6)   Han boede her *ikke* længe, *vel*?
        (=standard negation)
        (He didn't live here long, did he?)

(7a)   Han boede her indtil for *ikke* så længe siden, *ikke*?
        (<> standard negation)
        (He lived here until not very long ago, didn't he?)

(7b) * Han boede her indtil for *ikke* så længe siden, *vel*?
        (He lived here until not very long ago, did he?)

Beside standard negation we find the so-called 'standard equivalent negation'. It occurs in sentences which respond positively to the above-mentioned tests, but where the negation element does not occur independently. Examples of this are inherently negated elements, such as *ingen* (*no/no one*), *aldrig* (*never*) and *hverken..eller* (*neither..nor*).

Standard negation is used in both contrastive and non-contrastive negation. Here only non-contrastive negation is dealt with, as contrastive negation requires a treatment of non-basic coordination, for which EUROTRA doesn't have any principled theory yet. Some of the following examples can, however, be interpreted as instances of contrastive negation, but this has no consequences for our basic assumptions.

3. Negation scope in view of translation

There are several reasons why the calculation of negation scope is a relevant issue in an MT system. One of the major reasons concerns the fact that some languages place the negation element in close accordance with the intended negation scope, whereas other languages allow ambiguities. Consider the following sentence:

(8) *Hun har ikke læst mange bøger om emnet* - faktisk har hun slet ikke læst nogen.
(She hasn't read many books on the subject - in fact she has read none.)

(9) *Hun har ikke læst mange bøger om emnet* - selvom hun allerede har læst en hel del.
(She hasn't read many books on the subject - although she has already read quite a number.)

The sentence in italics is ambiguos with respect to negation scope, as can be seen from the different continuations. This difference can be elicited in Danish using the more common cleft-construction:

(10) Der/det er *ikke mange bøger*, hun har læst
(There are/it is not many books she has read)

(11) Der er *mange bøger*, hun *ikke* har læst
(There are many books she hasn't read)

In German, scope is more strongly indicated through the placement of the negation element. Therefore the italicized sentence in (8) and (9) will have the following two translations according to the two interpretations:

(12) Sie hat *nicht viele Bücher* gelesen

(13) Sie hat *viele Bücher nicht* gelesen

In view of passivization it is furthermore necessary to know whether the constituent candidating for subject function in a passive derivation is inside or outside the scope of negation in the source language. Consider:

(12) Sie hat *nicht viele Bücher* gelesen
(=> *Not many books* have been read by her)

(13) Sie hat *viele Bücher nicht* gelesen
(=> *Many books* haven*'t* been read by her)

In order to produce adequate translations of negated sentences, negation scope must be calculated for a wide range of the constituents of the sentence. As this is a very hard task - especially for adverbials - only NPs in the abovementioned functions are considered here.

4. Calculating negation scope

The scope of negation is determined on syntactic and semantic grounds. From a procedural point of view the calculation proceeds in two steps. The syntactic criteria are applied first during analysis of the constituent structure of the sentence. The semantic criteria are applied during the following deep syntactic analysis and will only affect constituents which have not been assigned a scope value during syntactic analysis. For a description of the EUROTRA stratificational approach, cf. *Studies in Machine Translation and Natural Language Processing*, 1991.

4.1 Syntactic aspects

The syntactic constraints for calculating negation scope are purely positional ones operating on the surface structure of the sentence. The operation they perform is analogous to the determination of quantifier scope in standard logic, stating that an element has scope over elements to its right and is itself inside the scope of elements to its left.

Constraint 1: An NP immediately following the negation element is obligatorily negated.

(14) Han forstod *ikke problemet*
(He didn't understand the problem)

(15) *Ikke ham* har hun givet pengene
(Not to him did she give the money)

In these examples the constituents *problemet* and *ham* are interpreted as being inside the scope of negation. For difficulties in applying this constraint to Danish in general see section 5.

Constraint 2: An NP occurring to the left of the negation element will be outside the scope of negation.

(14) *Han* forstod *ikke* problemet
(He didn't understand the problem)

(16) *Jeg* hilste *ikke* på nogen
(I din't say Hello to anybody)

(17) *Nogle* hilste *jeg ikke* på
(Somebody I didn't say hello to)

The examples (16) and (17) are expecially instructive. In the case of the quantifier *nogen* the plural form is morphologically determined by the scope of negation. The plural form occurring inside the scope of negation must be realized as *nogen* while the same quantifier occurring outside the scope of negation, must be realized as *nogle*.

The principle that elements to the left of the negation element are outside the scope of negation is correlated to the general information structure of the sentence. Usually, thematic elements which tend to be contextually 'given', occur to the left in the sentence and it is unusual to negate thematic, contextually bound elements. On the contrary, the negated elements are usually rhematic. This analysis is supported by certain word order regularities in Danish, as shown in:

(18) Hun gav *ikke postbudet* pengene
((lit.) She gave not the postman the money
She didn't give the money to the postman)

(19) Hun gav *ham ikke* pengene
((lit.) She gave him not the money
She didn't give him the money)

In Danish main clauses with the verb in simplex form, a full NP must occur to the right of the negation element (example (18)), while a pronominal anaphor (example (19)) must occur to the left (cf. Togeby 1989, p. 108). This could be explained by the fact that a pronominal anaphor necessarily refers to contextually given information which in the unmarked case tends not to be negated. On these grounds the position to the right of the negation element could be characterized as 'potentially inside the scope of negation'.

Constraint 3: An NP which is dominated and preceeded by the negation element can be inside or outside the scope of negation - or ambiguos between the two - depending on the semantic properties of the NP, which will be illustrated below.

4.2 Semantic aspects
4.2.1 Referential classification of NPs

In order to clarify the semantic aspects of scope calculation it is useful to divide all NPs into different classes according to their referential properties. Schematically the picture looks like this:

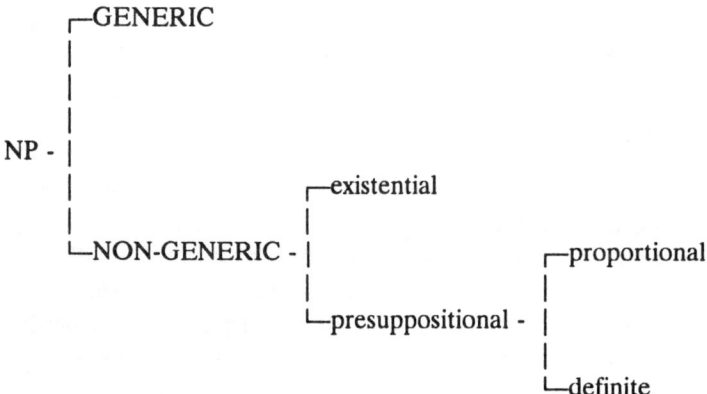

The main distinction concerns the genericness of the noun. Generic use is here understood as a reference to a set of properties which are common to all the individuals to which a given name can apply. As EUROTRA as yet does not have any 'legislation' on how to distinguish generic and non-generic NPs (which is partly due to the fact that EUROTRA does not look beyond the sentence boundary) only non-generic NPs are treated here.

In the field of non-generic NPs we distinguish 'existential' and 'presuppositional' NPs. Existential NPs are those which introduce new discourse entities, while presuppositional ones establish reference to an existing discourse entity or discourse set. A presuppositional NP can be either 'proportional' or 'definite'. 'Proportional' NPs introduce a subset within an exististing discourse set, while 'definite' NPs refer to existing discourse entities or sets.

The most tricky distinction here is the distinction between the proportional and the existential reading of an NP as many quantified NPs can receive both interpretations out of context. Consider the following examples from Loebner (1987), who speaks of a cardinal and a quantificational reading.

(20) When I entered the store, nobody was there except an older lady waiting and a man cleaning the windows. Finally, after a couple of minutes, *some salesmen walked in*.

(21) Lunchtime is from 12.30 p.m. to 1 p.m. As usual *the salesmen* met in the cafeteria. As there were no customers anyway at this time of the day they did not care too much to get back to the store in

time. At 1 o'clock, *some salesmen walked in*, but the rest stayed behind in the cafeteria.

In the first piece of text *some salesmen* allows only an existential reading, as a new discourse entity is introduced. In the second, instead, *some salesmen* introduces a subset of an already existing discourse set, so we are dealing with the proportional reading. The crucial differences between the two readings can be summarized as follows:

EXISTENTIAL	PROPORTIONAL
Head noun referentially new	Head noun referentially given
Partitive paraphrase impossible	Partitive paraphrase possible
* *Some of the salesmen*	*Some of the salesmen*
Determiner denotes the whole denotation of the head noun	Determiner denotes part of the denotation of the head noun

In case of quantifiers which allow both an existential and a proportional interpretation a distinction can only be made on contextual grounds. This is at present not possible in the EUROTRA analysis grammars. In Danish, however, it is possible to establish a distinction on syntactic grounds if the quantified NP is the subject of the sentence. If the existential reading is at stake, the subject NP will occur with the particle *der*, as in:

(22)   Endelig, efter et par minutter, kom *der nogle forretningsfolk* ind.
       ((lit.) Finally, after a couple of minutes, walked there some salesmen in.
       Finally, after a couple of minutes, some salesmen walked in.)

While no particle is required in the proportional reading (Cf. (21) for the appropriate context):

(23)   Klokken et kom *nogle forretningsfolk* ind, mens resten blev tilbage i cafeteria'et.
       (At 1 o'clock, some salesmen walked in, but the rest stayed) behind in the cafeteria.

If the NP is the object, only the context will identify the appropriate reading. Consequently, the parser has to produce two analyses, one with an existential and one with a proportional reading.

4.2.2 Referential properties and negation scope

The outlined classification of NPs according to their referential properties is correlated to the scope of negation in the following ways.

i): An NP that introduces a new discourse referent cannot occur outside the scope of negation. This means that an existential NP is always interpreted as being inside the scope of negation.

(24)　Der står *ikke* nogen *cykel* i gården
　　　(There is no bike in the yard)

(25)　Hun har *ikke* købt *en bog*
　　　(She has not bought a book)

Actually one should say that no introduction of discourse entities can occur within the scope of negation. Consider:

(26)　John har købt *en cykel*. *Den* var ret dyr.
　　　(John has bought a bike. It was rather expensive.)

(27)*/?　John har *ikke* købt *en cykel*. *Den* var for dyr.
　　　(John hasn't bought a bike. It was too expensive.)

Even though it is possible to think of a possible context for (27) it must be considered an incoherent text in isolation. The sentence would however be quite acceptable if the second clause contained a plural anaphor. Cf.

(28)　John har *ikke* købt *en cykel*. *De* var for dyre.
　　　(John hasn't bought a bike. They were too expensive.)

So even within the scope of negation existential NPs do introduce something, even though it is hard to establish exactly what this is.

ii): A proportional NP can be either inside or outside the scope of negation. Cf.

(29)　Hun talte *ikke* med *mange af lingvisterne*
　　　(She didn't talk to many of the linguists)

which is ambiguos between the following two interpretations:

(30) Der/det var *ikke mange af lingvisterne*, hun talte med.
(There were not many of the linguists, she talked to.)

(31) Der var *mange af lingvisterne*, hun *ikke* talte med.
(There were many of the linguists, she did not talk to.)

The difference is clear if the negation scope has consequences for the realization of the quantifier:

(32) Hun talte *ikke* med *nogen* af lingvisterne
(She didn't talk to any of the linguists)
- NP inside negation scope

(33) Hun talte *ikke* med *nogle* af lingvisterne
(She didn't talk to some of the linguists)
- NP outside negation scope

It is however the case that such a quantified NP can only be inside the scope of negation if the quantifier itself can be negated. Cf.

Ikke mange af lingvisterne...
(Not many of the linguists...)

- *mange (many)* can be inside the scope of negation.

* *Ikke adskillige* af lingvisterne...
(Not several of the linguists...)

- *adskillige (several)* can never be inside the scope of negation.

It is not quite clear exactly which semantic properties of the quantifiers determine whether they can be negated or not. So instead of a semantic characterization we use the 'ad-hoc'-attribute 'msnegable', stating whether the quantifier is morphosyntactically negatable in preverbal position or not. The consequence of this is that all quantifiers have to be marked for morphosyntactic negatability in the lexicon.

iii): A definite NP can only be outside the scope of negation, as shown by the fact that a definite NP can always be referred to anaphorically.

(34) Hun talte med *lingvisten*. Han kom lige forbi.
(She spoke to the linguist. He passed her.)

(35)   Hun talte *ikke* med *lingvisten*. Han havde for travlt.
       (She didn't speak to the linguist. He was too busy.)

4.2.3 Relevant attribute/value pairs

To summarize: In order to determine the scope of negation the following attribute/value pairs are relevant. The semicolon indicates disjunction.

1. Is the NP existential or presuppositional?
   {presup = yes;no}

2. Is the NP definite?
   {definite = yes;no}

3. Can the NP be morphosyntactically negated?
   {msnegable = yes;no}

Through various combinations of these features all the abovementioned subclasses of NPs can be described. A proportional NP will be marked by the features {presup=yes, definite=no}, a definite NP by the features {presup=yes, definite=yes} and an existential NP by the feature {presup=no}. All these values have to be calculated during analysis. It is however possible to establish the following implication rules:

```
{presup=no}      => {definite=no}
{definite=yes}   => {presup=yes}
{definite=yes}   => {msnegable=no}
{msnegable=yes}  => {definite=no}
```

On the basis of the features presuppositionality, definiteness and msnegability we get the following possible combinations concerning calculation of negation scope:

	presup	definite	msnegable	scope
1)	yes	yes	yes	(impossible)
2)	yes	yes	no	only outside
3)	yes	no	yes	inside or outside
4)	yes	no	no	only outside
5)	no	yes	yes	(impossible)
6)	no	yes	no	(impossible)
7)	no	no	yes	only inside
8)	no	no	no	neither inside nor outside

As can be seen from the scheme, some combinations are logically impossible. So for example it is impossible for an NP to be non-presuppositional and definite at the same time. It might seem a little puzzling that the first combination is excluded as impossible considering the fact that you can certainly say:

(36)   *Ikke ham* har hun givet pengene
       (Not to him did she give the money)

However, this is considered an instance of contrastive negation and contrastive negation seems to permit more subtle scoping phenomena modifying the presuppositional content of the utterance. Furthermore, this kind of negation will be captured by the abovementioned positional constraints (constraint 1) which are applied before the semantic analysis.

Exemplification:

2) *Hun*   only outside negation scope
   (she)
   lingvisten
   (the linguist)

3) *Mange af bøgerne*   either inside or outside negation scope
   (many of the books)
   (proportional reading)

4) *Adskillige af bøgerne*   only outside negation scope
   (several of the books)
   (proportional reading)

7) *En bog*   only inside negation scope
   (a book)

8) *Adskillige bøger*   neither inside nor outside negation scope
   (several books)
   (existential reading)

The consequence of the statement in 8 is that the existential reading of *adskillige* cannot occur in negated sentences at all. Cf.

(37) * Der leger *ikke adskillige* børn i haven
       (There are not several children playing in the garden)

As can be seen from the diagram, ambiguity occurs in the case of quantifiers with a proportional reading. In that case it is necessary to produce two analyses, yielding two translations into say German, from which one is the right one. If the NP containing the quantifier furthermore is ambiguos between the existential and the proportional reading (which is usually the case in Danish when the NP appears in object function with an indefinite head noun), three analyses will be produced. Cf.

(38) Hun har *ikke* læst *mange bøger*
      (She hasn't read many books)

   a) existential reading, inside negation scope
   b) proportional reading, inside negation scope
   c) proportional reading, outside negation scope

4.2.4 Exemplification of scope calculation

Whether an NP is inside or outside the scope of negation is indicated with the feature {sNEG=yes;no}. 'sNEG' stands for 'semantically negated'.

1: {presup=yes, definite=yes, msnegable=no} =>
    {sNEG=no}

These values are attributed to:

   a) NPs with definite article
   b) NPs with demonstrative article
   c) NPs with possessive phrases
      - NP in genitive
      - Possessive pronoun
   d) Proper names
   e) Personal and demonstrative pronouns

2: {presup=yes, definite=no, msnegable=yes} =>
    {sNEG=yes;no}

These values are attributed to quantified NPs with a presuppositional reading where the quantifier is marked for {msnegable=yes} in the lexicon.

(39) Hun har *ikke* læst *mange af bøgerne*
      (She hasn't read many of the books)

3: {presup=yes, definite=no, msnegable=no} =>
    {sNEG=no}

These values are attributed to quantified NPs with a presuppositional reading where the quantifier is marked for {msnegable=no} in the lexicon.

(40)   Hun har *ikke* læst *adskillige af bøgerne*
       (She hasn't read several of the books)

4:    {presup=no, definite=no, msnegable=yes} =>
      {sNEG=yes}

These values are attributed to:

a) NPs with indefinite article
b) NPs without article
c) Quantified NPs with existential reading where the quantifier is marked for {msnegable=yes} in the lexicon.

(41)   Der er *ikke* lagt *mange øller* på køl
       (There are not many beers in the fridge)

5. Applying these strategies to Danish

In the preceding sections I have sketched the general strategies used to calculate the scope of negation adopted in the EUROTRA machine translation system. As mentioned in the beginning, this strategy is meant to be 'euroversal', which means that it is adopted by all language groups in their analysis grammars. Applying this strategy to Danish has called for some changes in the Danish implementation, however.

Consider firstly the second syntactic constraint: 'An NP to the left of the negation element is obligatorily outside the scope of negation.'

(42)   Hun har heller *ikke en øl*
       (She doesn't have a beer, either)

It is however quite possible in Danish to move the object into the socalled fundament field (the first place before the finite verb).

(43)   *En øl* har hun heller *ikke*
       (A beer, she doesn't have either)

En øl (a beer) is not removed from the scope of negation for that reason. Consider furthermore:

(44)   Hun har *ingen bøger*
       (She has no books)

(45)   *Bøger* har hun *ingen* af
       (Books she has none)

This last construction is also possible in German:

(46)   *Bücher* hat sie *keine*

Thus for this constraint to apply properly we have to presuppose a 'normal' word order with the subject in the fundament field, which is also the most common word order in Danish.

As for the first syntactic constraint: 'An NP immediately to the right of the negation element is obligatorily inside the scope of negation', this needs a prerequisite as well. This constraint works well for German:

(47)   Sie hat dem Briefträger das Geld *nicht* gegeben

(48)   Sie hat *nicht dem Briefträger* das Geld gegegen

But applying it to Danish has some unwanted consequences.

(18)   Hun gav *ikke postbudet* pengene
       ((lit.) She gave not the postman the money
       She didn't give the money to the postman)

In this sentence *postbudet* (*the postman*) will be interpreted as being within the scope of negation because of its position immediately to the right of the negation element. If however the verb is realized in the perfect:

(49)   Hun har *ikke* givet *postbudet* pengene
       (She has not given the postman the money)

postbudet (*the postman*) is suddenly outside the scope of negation as the infinite verb has come in between the negation element and the NP, which is definite. This would lead us to the unacceptable conclusion that the choice of tense has consequences for the intended scope of negation. So here we need the restriction that the NP in question must appear in the fundament field (=preverbal position):

(50)   *Ikke postbudet* gav hun pengene
       (Not to the postman did she give the money)

This however reveals another more serious implication of this strategy for calculating the scope of negation.

In sentence (49) *postbudet* (*the postman*) is interpreted as being outside the scope of negation, as it is a definite, presuppositional NP standing to the right of the negation element. In sentence (50) however the very same NP will be interpreted as being inside the scope of negation as it stands to the immediate right of the negation element - in spite of its semantic properties which in (49) prevented it from being inside the negation scope. This implies that the syntactic criteria which are based on the position of the constituents in question, always prevail on the semantic criteria. This might be the case, but it raises the fundamental question of what it means to be inside the scope of negation, when an NP in one situation is excluded from being inside the scope of negation because of its semantic properties while it can be inside the negation scope in another case. This problem crops up because the linear structuring of the sentence here is dealt with as a syntactic phenomenon. Conceiving of the linear structuring of the sentence and the text as an integral part of a discourse component, the outlined priority of positional constraints may well be justified. But even so a clarification of this particular interaction is needed. In any case these problems deserve further study.

References

Grundzüge einer deutschen Grammatik (1980). Von einem Autorenkollektiv. Berlin.

Hajicova, E. (1977) 'Focus and negation', in: Zampolli (ed), *Linguistic Structures Precessing. Fundamental Studies in Computer Science*, vol. 5. Amsterdam /New York / Oxford.

Halliday, M. A. K. (1975) 'Language structure and language function', in: Lyons, John (ed), *New horizons in linguistics. Aylesbury/Bucks*.

Hoekstra, Heleen (1985) 'The final truth about negation', in: *The Eurotra Newsletter*, Number 15, April / 1985

Hoekstra, Heleen (1990) 'Negation', in: *The Eurotra Reference Manual. 7.0.* (Internal Document, CEC/Luxembourg).

Jackendoff, R. S. (1972) *Semantic interpretation in Generative Grammar.* Cambridge Mass. / London.

Klima, E. S. (1964) 'Negation in English', in: Fodor & Katz (eds) *The structure of Language*. Prentice-Hall, Englewood Cliffs, N. J.

Loebner, S. (1987) 'Natural Language and Generalized Quantifier Theory', in: P. Gärdenfors (ed) *Generalized Quantifiers*. Dordrecht.

Payne, J. R. (1985) 'Negation', in: Shopen (ed) *Language Typology and Syntactic description*, vol. 1 (clause structure) Cambridge University press.

Studies in Machine Translation and Natural Language Processing (1991), Vol 1: *The Eurotra linguistic specifications*. Luxembourg.

Togeby, Ole (1989) *Sprogbrugsfunktionen*. Unpublished Working Paper.

Verb Valency and Automatic Text Processing

Michael Herslund and Finn Sørensen
Copenhagen Business School

1. Introduction

The initial observation which motivates our concept of verb valency is the fact that verbs denote relations: the only way of conceptualising the denotation of a verb is as a relation between entities. From this follows the first dichotomy which is reflected in language:

- relations in reality are between entities, in language between **arguments**
- relations can, as can entities, be modified (e.g. a movement can be fast or slow, etc.), in language by **modifiers**.

The entities and the relations between them, modified or not, can be placed upon a scene and/or be globally modified, so we get four classes of linguistic expressions (clause constituents): the bound expressions, i.e. expressions determined by the lexical content of the verb, arguments and modifiers, and the free expressions, i.e. the expressions which combine with any verb regardless of its lexical specifications:

	Bound	*Free*
(1) *Argument*	Complement (Valent)	Adjunct
Modifier	Bound Adverb	Free Adverb

2. Complements and adjuncts

In this context we concentrate on the Arguments and have nothing further to say about the Modifiers. Among the Complements, we distinguish three functions, viz. S(ubject), O(bject) and A(dject), earlier labelled Indirect object, and two kinds of clause structure, viz. transitive and intransitive (for further details, see e.g. Herslund 1988b and Herslund and Sørensen (forthcoming); the bibliography contains complete references to our other works on the valency approach). One fundamental problem for any valency approach is how one can properly distinguish between Complements and Adjuncts in processing a text. We present below some cases where the problem becomes acute because the two classes of clause constituents are structurally indistinguishable, i.e. they have identical structural expressions. This happens most conspicuously, in the modern European languages, in the case of PPs. And the problem is especially urgent in Danish with its pervasive use of PPs.

What makes the problem difficult is the fact that the same PP sometimes is a Complement (dependent upon the verb), sometimes an Adjunct (a clause constituent), and furthermore, sometimes a constituent of an NP inside which it can have the status either as a Complement or as an Adjunct. So in processing a PP one has really four possibilities to take into account:

(2)

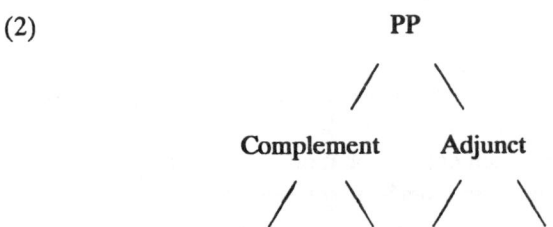

Add to this that there may be holes in a given structure, i.e. an expected, lexically determined Complement is not realised. We do not, in fact, believe that there is such a thing as an obligatory Complement.

Before turning to a closer description of the Adject relation, in section 3., we present two problematic cases, without, however, suggesting any solutions:

- the distinction between verbal and nominal valency
- the systematic alternation between a direct and a prepositional object found with many verbs in Danish.

2.1 Verbal and nominal valency

The first case is a charateristic class of constructions, the so-called **Support Verb Constructions**: in these constructions, the real predicate is an NP whereas the verb is a rather colourless carrier of verbal morphemes such as tense and mood; in a sense, the verb only serves to conjugate the predicative noun. One problem with such constructions is the fact that 'Support Verb' does not define a **class of verbs**, but rather a **class of uses** of certain verbs. So it is not sufficient to refer to a list of verbs in order to identify the constructions.

One charateristic feature of such constructions seems to be that they allow a double analysis, i.e. a PP can be viewed as either dependent upon a noun (be an NP constituent), or as dependent upon the complex Verb + NP, cf. (3) and (4):

(3) a. Per har lavet en tegning *af en havfrue*.
    (Per has made a drawing of a mermaid)

        b. Det er en tegning *af en havfrue*, Per har lavet.
           (It is a drawing of a mermaid Per has made)
        c. Det er *af en havfrue*, Per har lavet en tegning.
           (It is of a mermaid that Per has made a drawing)
(4)   a. Per har købt en tegning *af en havfrue*.
           (Per has bought a drawing of a mermaid)
        b. Det er en tegning *af en havfrue*, Per har købt.
           (It is a drawing of a mermaid Per has bought)
  * c. Det er *af en havfrue*, Per har købt en tegning.
           (It is of a mermaid that Per has bought a drawing)

As can be seen, there are two clefting possibilities in (3), with the verb *lave* (make): in (3) b., the O *en tegning af en havfrue* is isolated from the verb *har lavet* (the "normal" construction); in (3) c., the PP *af en havfrue* is isolated from the "verb" *har lavet en tegning* (the support verb construction). But in (4) c., the PP *af en havfrue* cannot be isolated leaving *har købt en tegning* behind as a complex verb; *købe* (buy) cannot function as a support verb. We disregard of course here the irrelevant, but grammatical reading of (4)c., where the mermaid sells the drawing.

On the other hand, single constituents can be extracted from complex NPs provided these NPs are marked as such by stranding the preposition:

(3)   c'. Det er en havfrue, Per har lavet en tegning af.
(4)   c'. Det er en havfrue, Per har købt en tegning af.

So in processing a sequence of the form ...**V + NP + PP** several possible analyses present themselves.

2.2 Prepositional objects

The second case is the alternation between a direct and a prepositional object found with a large number of verbs in Danish (see Durst-Andersen and Herslund (forthcoming)). The alternation is connected with changes in the semantics of the verb: the direct object construction conveys an action reading, i.e. the action is completed, whereas the prepositional construction conveys an activity, or a process, reading, i.e. the intended action is incomplete, as in (5):

(5)   a. Jeg har skrevet en roman.
          (I have written a novel)
      b. Jeg har skrevet på en roman.
          (I have been writing a novel)

With structures containing one of the verbs which partake in the alternation ...**V + NP** ~ ...**V + PP**, how can one know whether a given sequence containing a PP has the structure (6) a. or (6) b., a structure with a hole in it?

(6) a. ...V + PP
    b. ...V (NP)-Ø + PP

How in other words are we to interpret examples like (7), or (8) containing an intransitive verb which can be "transitivised" by way of a prepositional construction?

(7)   Jeg vil læse på Raskolnikov i weekenden.
      (I'll do some reading on Raskolnikov this weekend)

(8) a. Hun arbejder på Det kgl. Bibliotek.
       (She works in the Royal Library)
    b. Han arbejder på et stillads.
       (He works on a scaffold)

One could in fact imagine that *Raskolnikov* is the name of a bar, in order to get a locative reading corresponding to (6) b., or that *Det kgl. Bibliotek* denotes a model of the library, or that someone is engaged in constructing a scaffold rather than working on one, in order to get non-locative readings corresponding to (6) a., rather than the immediately more attractive locative readings. The locative readings can of course in all cases be made explicit by way of an adverbial specifier in the PP, cf. (9):

(9) a. Jeg vil læse *inde/henne* på Raskolnikov i weekenden.
    b. Hun arbejder *inde/henne* på Det kgl. Bibliotek.
    c. Han arbejder *oppe* på et stillads

which can only have the locative meaning. In the same way, the very lexical material of the PP will often suffice to disambiguate, cf. (10):

(10)   De må ikke forstyrre Mozart. Han komponerer på sit requiem.
       (You can't disturb Mozart. He is composing his Requiem)

just as *Raskolnikov* in (7) will tend to favour the non-locative reading.

But examples like these show that the lexical specifications of verbs, their valency, often do not suffice to ensure the correct analysis of sentences. The question is then whether the more extended context of a complete text is really enough.

3. Valency and text processing

Having presented above our conception of valency and some problems it must face somehow, we now proceed to illustrate why this conception can be used in text processing. Some of our proposals have already been implemented in the interface described in Hansen and Vikner 1989.

A text can be regarded as a sequence of sentences. Each sentence gives information about some situation, and the conjunction of the information given by the sentences of a text is the information of the text about the relevant situations.

To understand a text can be considered to be the state of an agent (a human being or a computer) in which the agent on exposure to a text has the information carried by the text, i.e. the relation illustrated in (11):

(11) *understand* (**Agent, Text, Information, Situation**)

From this picture of understanding, and thus also of text processing, it should be clear that the step from Text to Information is crucial.It is also at this point our conception of valency becomes useful. Why that is so is explicated below.

3.1 From valency schemes to infons

The relevance of valency to information can be explicated in the following way. A verb is a structured unit which can occur in different forms in a text. One af the components af a verb is its valency scheme. In a text then, the processor has access to verb forms, and through verb forms to verbs and their valency schemes. For each verb there is furthermore a particular relation of the same structural type as that defined by its valency scheme. That a relation is of the same structural type as a valency scheme is defined by the following relations between syntactic valency schemes (to the left of the arrow) and relations (to the right of the arrow):

(12) a. $V(S) \rightarrow R(s:X)$
 b. $V(S,O) \rightarrow R(s:X, o:Y)$
 c. $V(S,A) \rightarrow R(s:X, a:Y)$
 d. $V(S,O,A) \rightarrow R(s:X, o:Y, a:Z)$

In (12), V is a variable over verbs. The letters S, O, and A are the functional labels subject, object, and adject which we introduced in section 2. R is a variable over relations. At the lefthand side of the arrow, the functional labels name a position which can be assigned constituents of different types. At the righthand side of the arrow, the functional labels name slots which can be assigned entities of the different types. X, Y, Z are variables over entities, i.e. individuals, properties and so forth. To sum up, the presented conception of valency brings us from verb forms, over verbs, to valency schemes, and finally to relations having one of the forms sketched in (12). But - as is well known, i.e from Barwise and Perry 1983, Cooper 1987 or Devlin 1991 - a relation with its arguments constitutes a unit which, as the basic part of an infon, represents information about some situation, and thus functions as a classifier of the situation talked about. Given a text containing a verb form, valency thus acts as a tool for the text processor in its search for the information associated with the verb form. The crucial step in this process is the step depicted in (12).

3.2 Technical remarks
When we talk about valency we often use only the forms at the lefthand side of the arrow in (12). This 'conflated' way of representing the structure of a verb is innocent because the context will show whether we focus on the syntactic or the semantic side of a particular problem. However, it is important to stress - in this text processing context - that the conflated representation means that we take it as a fact that the relation associated with a verb is structurally identical to the verb and its syntactic valency scheme. This assumption implies in particular that the relation associated with a verb has the number and the labelled kinds of arguments it has by definition, whether a particular use of the verb in a sentence has all its labelled positions filled in or not. The correlations expressed in (12) are thus a more explicit way to say what we usually say in a 'conflated' way. This general remark should make it clear that we do not follow the standard procedure in model-theoretic semantics where a predicate symbol must be combined with a fixed number of expressed syntactic arguments and where such a symbol cannot be interpreted if it has not been applied to the right number of arguments.

We also confess that we do not follow the standard praxis of using real numbers, i.e. the set $A=\{1,2,3\}$ as labels of the argument slots. From a purely formal point of view, our choice of the set $F=\{S,O,A\}$ and the definition of the possible forms given in (12), has been guided by the fact that we end up with a richer typology of forms. With the set F, we thus obtain both $V(S,O)$ and $V(S,A)$, while the set A only gives rise to the binary form $V(1,2)$. Furthermore, we want to be able to pick out adjects as a particular type of argument whether they occur in a binary or 3-ary structure. But this seems impossible or at least very difficult if it is only possible to refer to either 'argument n', type of syntactic constituents or type of semantic entities. The important point in connection with adjects is their function within the structure they are part of. That is what we capture in a simple way by labelling both positions and slots with functional labels. For some discussion of the use of functional labels in the difinition of the valency (or the arity) of relations, see Sørensen 1990b.

3.3 Valency and the flow of information
So far, we have illustrated why valency is important for the function of a text processor by helping it with the extraction of information from a text. We also think that our way of looking at valency combined with some ideas of the situation theoretic approach to language allows us to capture some of the flow of information which takes place when a language is used. In fact, we claim that there is a general constraint on all situations supporting infons containing

arguments assigned to slots labelled adject. What that means is explicated below.

Consider first the following sentences:

(13) a. Peter virker *træt*.
(Peter looks tired)
b. Peter er træt.
(Peter is tired)
(14) a. Peter bor *i London*.
(Peter lives in London)
b. Peter er i London.
(Peter is in London)
(15) a. Ce livre appartient *à Pierre*.
(This book belongs to Pierre)
b. Ce livre est à Pierre.
(This book is Pierre's)
(16) a. Peter gør mig *gal*.
(Peter makes me mad)
b. Jeg er gal.
(I am mad)
(17) a. Peter lægger bogen på *bordet*.
(Peter puts the book upon the table)
b. Bogen er på bordet.
(The book is on the table)
(18) a. Peter giver *Marie* bogen.
(Peter gives Marie the book)
b. Marie har bogen.
(Marie has the book)

The (a)-sentences illustrate constructions containing adjects (the underlined constituents). All these adjects are arguments in the valency framework assumed above. Besides being arguments of the verbs, the adjects also enter into a specific relation with either the subject (in binary constructions) or the object (in the 3-ary constructions). Given these observations, the problem is how we can handle them in a satisfactory way. Our proposals are as follows. First we introduce the relational parameter Loc which is binary, locational and stative. The parameter Loc denotes binary relations, but only that sort of binary relations which are both stative and locational. That a relation is stative means that the situation supporting the infon containing the relation is a state. That a relation is locational means that the denotation of one of its arguments is predicated to be located somehow at or within the domain of the denotation of the other argument. Our claim is thus that Loc is an explication of the adject relation, and that the information given by the (b)-sentences in (13)-(18) is an instantiation of Loc. Notice that Loc as a parameter does not need to have its potential arguments assigned to specific roles. Given the classificatory properties of Loc, there are two possibilities. Either the adject relation predicates something which corresponds with the (b)-examples of (13), (14), (16) and (17). Or it predicates something which corresponds with the (b)-sentences in (15) and (18).

Having defined the adject relation in terms of Loc, we propose the following general constraint:

(19) A situation s supporting an infon i involves a situation s' supporting an infon i' under the condition that i contains an adject, that i' contains Loc, and that the argument slots of Loc are assigned arguments as illustrated above.

This constraint makes the prediction that whenever an agent uses a sentence containing an adject and thus gives some information about some situation s, he also gives the information represented by the adject relation and illustrated by the (b)-sentences in (13)-(18). This latter information may be about s or some other situation s', depending to a high degree on the aspectual properties of the sentence used by the agent. Notice that (19) gives rise to flow of information. This flow of information should not be produced directly by the text processor, but may be the result of applying 'general text knowledge' to the output of the text processor. As the result depends on the notion of an adject, we think that also at this level our conception of valency is useful to someone working with text processing.

Bibliography

Barwise, J. and J. Perry (1983) *Situations and Attitudes*. The MIT Press, Cambridge, Mass.

Cooper, R. (1987) *Introduction to Situation Semantics*. Stanford University, Stanford.

Devlin, K. (1991) *Logic and Information*. Cambridge University Press, Cambridge.

Durst-Andersen, P. and M. Herslund (forthcoming) 'Prepositional Objects in Danish', in: *Papers from the 13th Scandinavian Conference of Linguistics*. Roskilde University Center.

Hansen, S.L. and C. Vikner (1989) *FAGFLADE. The Initial Phase of a Project in Natural Language Interpretation*. LAMBDA 11, Institut for Datalingvistik, Copenhagen Business School.

Herslund, M. (1982) *Dativ. En syntaktisk-semantisk analyse af à N strukturer på fransk*. RIDS 100, Romansk Institut, University of Copenhagen.

Herslund, M. (1986) 'The Double Object Construction in Danish', in: Hellan and Koch Christensen (eds): *Topics in Scandinavian Syntax*, 125-147. Reidel, Dordrecht.

Herslund, M. (1988a) *Le datif en français*. Editions Peeters, Louvain-Paris.

Herslund, M. (1988b) 'On Valence and Grammatical Relations', in: Sørensen (ed): *Valence, Three Studies on the Linking Power of Verbs*, 3-34. Copenhagen Studies in Language, CEBAL Series 11.

Herslund, M. (1989) 'Les relations syntaxiques dans une approche valentielle'. Communication au XIXe Congrès international de linguistique et philologie romanes, Santiago de Compostela.

Herslund, M. (1990) 'Les verbes inaccusatifs comme problème lexicographique', in: *Cahiers de lexicologie* 56-57, 35-44.

Herslund, M. og F. Sørensen (1982) 'Syntaks og leksikologi. Indledning til en valensgrammatisk analyse af dansk og fransk', in: *SAML* 9, 33-83. IAML, University of Copenhagen.

Herslund, M. og F. Sørensen (1985) *De franske verber. En valens-grammatisk fremstilling. I. Verbernes syntaks*. Romansk Institut, University of Copenhagen. (2nd edition 1990, Samfundslitteratur, Copenhagen).

Herslund, M. og F. Sørensen (1987) *De franske verber 2. En valensgrammatisk fremstilling II. Klassifikation*. Samfundslitteratur, Copenhagen.

Herslund, M. og F. Sørensen (1991) 'A Valence Based Theory of Grammatical Relations', in: Falster Jakobsen and Harder (eds): *Function and Expression in Functional Grammar*. Mouton-de Gruyter, Berlin.

Sørensen, F. (1983) 'Un drôle d'object indirect', in: Spore et alii (eds): *Actes du VIIIe Congrès des Romanistes Scandinaves*, 351-359. Odense University Press, Odense.

Sørensen, F. (1986) 'Passivkonstruktioner er prædikatskonstruktioner', in: Davidsen-Nielsen og Sørensen (eds): *Festskrift til Jens Rasmussen*, 230-249. CEBAL 8. Copenhagen.

Sørensen, F. (1988) 'Indice d'infinitif ou préposition. Comment intégrer cette distinction dans un analyseur', in: Herslund et alii (eds): *Traditions et tendances nouvelles des études romanes au Danemark*, 223-233. Etudes Romanes de l'Université de Copenhague 31. Munksgaard, Copenhague.

Sørensen, F. (1990a) 'Om blive-passiver. En lokationsbaseret prædikatsanalyse', in: *LAMBDA* 16, 137-193. Institut for Datalingvistik, Copenhagen Business School.

Sørensen, F. (1990b) *Mærket Aritet*. Institut for Datalingvistik, Copenhagen Business School.

Sørensen, F. (1991) (med L. Denver og B. Lihn Jensen) 'The Passive Construction in Danish, Italian and Spanish', in: K.M. og O. Lauridsen (eds): *Contrastive Linguistics*, 19-49. Århus Business School.

Indefinite NPs in Legal Texts. An Application of Electronic Dictionaries in a Textlinguistic Study

Lita Lundquist
Copenhagen Business School

Introduction

The study which is reported below started out as a purely empirical analysis which aimed at testing how a given set of electronic dictionaries would function as a tool in investigating a specific and rather well delimited textlinguistic phenomenon.

The electronic dictionaries which I wanted to apply were designed and developed by the *Laboratoire d'Automatique Documentaire et Linguistique* (LADL). They had kindly been put at the disposal of the French Department of the Copenhagen Business School by the scientific director of the project, professor Maurice Gross, in an exchange of a corpus of French and English legal text (Dyrberg 1991). The specific textlinguistic phenomenon I decided to study was the use of *indefinite NPs* (indNP) in a small sample of four different types of legal texts in French from the above-mentioned corpus, namely a *law*, a *legal decision*, a *textbook* and a *legal article*. The four texts treated the same legal topic, namely contracts. Being rather atheoretical, at the outset, I contented myself with the rather coarse textlinguistic principle that indNP introduce new discourse referents in a mental representation of the text, whereas definite NPs maintain discourse referents. However, being somewhat sceptical about this - as it seemed to me - too idealistically clearcut distinction as to the function of the two types of determiners, I wanted on the one hand to see whether indNP assume other functions in a text, and on the other to show possible relationships between the use of indNP and different text types, i.e., different discourse worlds.

The electronic dictionaries

For some decades now, professor Maurice Gross and his "équipes" have been working on compiling a set of extremely comprehensive dictionaries of the French language [1]. The dictionairies are morphologically based, i.e., for each entry, they mark word class and inflection: gender, number, person, time, mood. A thorough description is given in Courtois and Silberztein: *Dictionnaires électroniques du français* (1990), so here I will restrict myself to

---

[1] So, for instance, DELAS, the dictionary of French words in their basic form, contains 80.000 entries, DELAF, containing the same words in all their morphological forms, contains 900.000 entries (june 1990).

Steen Jansen et al (eds): Computational Approaches to Text Understanding,
☉ Museum Tusculanum Press, Copenhagen 1992

enumerating the main points of interest for using the dictionaries as a tool for automatic analysis of texts. First, the dictionaries can be used to tag a text with morphological markings, and to establish a "local dictionary" for the text. The following is an example of a morphological tagging:

Ex. 1: '*Il* ((il Pro)) *arrive* ((arriver V3:P 1 s:P3s:s1s:S3s:Y2s)) *assez* ((assez Adv)) *souvent* ((souvent Adv)) *qu* ((qu Xin)) *'avant* ((avant Prép)) *la* ((la Dét)) *négociation* ((négociation N2 1:fs)) *contractuelle* ((contractuel A40:fs)) (contractuel N40;fs)), *des* ((des Dét)) *modèles* (modèle N1: mp) (modèle A31:mp:fp)(modeler V6:P2s: S2s)) ..... *soient* ((etre V2:S3p)) ... *élaborés* ((élaborer V3.Kmp (élaboré A32:mp))'.

Second, a text can be automatically marked for fixed expressions, via the "dictionnaire des mots composés", as shown in example 2 below:

Ex. 2: '... divers fournisseurs d'une <*société commerciale*> avaient souscrit une <*assurance crédit*> ...'

And third, it is possible with the help of the dictionaries and specific users' programs to set up "local grammars", i.e., strings which can search for combinations of words, word classes and inflections in a given sequence, which simulate the syntactic ordering of the linguistic elements. Example 3 presents a local grammar which searches out a combination of Noun + 'de' + Noun + the adjective 'contractuel':

ex 3: (<N>/de/<N>/<*contractuel*>).

The question I wanted to pose was whether these search strings could also be used to set up *local text grammars*, i.e., grammars which seek textual phenomena which often go beyond and across a sentence level. Being aware of a number of restrictions intrinsic to the LADL programs, first of all that they cannot transcend the sentence boundary, and secondly that they have no memory and no way of working with variables, I was nevertheless optimistic as to the possibility of elucidating the surroundings in which indNP appear in texts.

Below I present the different search procedures that I created in order to cast light on the function of indNP in legal texts, but let me first underline that my study of indNP was restricted to the use of NP introduced by 'un' and 'une', ("unNP"), that is NP in singular form only. The reason for this restriction in this rather preliminary study was pure convenience, the unNP being the only indNP that the computer could sort out unambiguously or quasi-unambiguously. So in the following, the reference to indNP includes unNP only.

The search procedures and their results
The first local grammar
The first local grammar aimed quite simply at extracting all occurrences of unNP in the four text samples. It was formulated in the following way:

Local grammar 1:
(un+une)/(<MOT>+<E>)/(<MOT>+<E>)/(<MOT>+<E>)/ <N>

This is to be read: find occurrences of 'un' or 'une' followed three times by either an arbitrary word (MOT) or ("+" = or) zero (E), followed by a noun (N): i.e., a unNP with up to three words between determiner and noun. The results from this initial search were rather neat and gave way first to some small, rudimentary statistics about the number of types and tokens of unNP in the four text types, and secondly to a first classification of their textual function.

The indNP appeared in the four texts with the following frequency, shown in relation to the frequency of defNP sing ('le N' and 'la N'):

Table 1.

	IndNP	*DefNP*
Law text (ca 1800 words)	18typ, 19tok	77typ, 92tok
Judgement (ca 310 words)	2typ, 4tok	13typ, 19tok
Text book (ca 1200 words)	16typ, 18tok	73typ, 78tok
Article (ca 1890 words)	53typ, 56tok	115typ, 121tok

Apart from the fact that defNP are by far more frequent in all the texts than indNP [2], it is to be noticed from this table that the legal article contained a very high number of indNP compared to the other text types (almost three times as many as the comparable law text), whereas the judgement contained very few, a fact which I will comment upon in the concluding remarks.

On the basis of a listing of the results, I could classify the function of indNP and exclude certain groups as being either not the indefinite article, at all, or not introducing discourse referents:

1. nominal use of 'un'/'une'. Example: 'l'une des deux lois'

2. frozen expressions. Examples: 'd'une certaine manière', 'un grand nombre', 'dans une assez large mesure'.

---

[2] The high frequency of defNP in texts - and the question of "where they are known from" - has led to a considerable amount of linguistic literature on the type of presupposed background knowledge encoded in determinedness.

3. 'un' and 'une' as numerals. Example: '... illustré par deux lois du 10 janvier 1978 et une loi du 13 juillet 1979'.

4. "anaphoric use", namely with a preposed "indefinite pronoun" such as 'pareil', 'tel', 'si'. Examples: 'une pareille réglementation', 'un tel accord', 'une si grande réduction'.

5. predicative use of indNP. Example: '... le droit commun ... qui présente ce caractère d'être un droit commun impératif'.

Restricting my analysis to the rest of the examples, I formulated a number of questions which I tried to elucidate with the help of new local grammars, namely:

1. In which syntactic functions do indNP appear?

2. Are certain verbs more disposed - via their semantic content - to be constructed with indNP than others?

3. Is there a special distribution of indNP with abstract versus concrete nouns?

4. Do indNP invite a specific or a non-specific reading?

5. How do the different functions of indNP correlate with text types?

The second local grammar
With a second grammar I tried to locate indNP in subject position, i.e., before a verb in a finite form. The grammar looked like this:

Local grammar 2:
(un+une)/(<MOT>+<E>)/(<MOT>+<E>)/(<MOT>+<E>)/<-N>/(<MOT>+<E>)/(<MOT>+<E>)/(<MOT>+<E>)/<V:P3>+-<V:I>+<V:S>+<V:J>+<V:F>+<V:C>)

This should be read in the following way: Look for indNP - allowing three arbitrary words between the determiner and the noun - followed by - again allowing the appearance of three arbitrary words - a verb in the present form third person (V:P3), or a verb in the imperfect form (V:I), or a verb in the present subjunctive form (V:S), or a verb in the "remote past" form (passé simple) (V:J), or a verb in the future form (V:F) or a verb in the conditional (V:C).

This grammar gave a very surprising result, one that was totally unreliable and with many errors. A short sample of the somewhat absurd results is shown below:

> *une oeuvre authentique*
> *une augmentation des charges dépassant très notablement les hausses*
> *une hausse de plus*
> *une périodicité égale*
> *une société mère et par ses filiales sont*
> *un grand nombre*
> *une assez large mesure*
> *une législation de plus en plus*
> *une manière plus approfondie le rôle*
> *un émane de la première Chambre*
> *un lien contractuel entre*
> *un simple droit de stationnement à ses risques*
> *Une société hôtelière réclamait paiement des sommes*
> *une faute lourde*

It appears from this list that errors are caused by the ambiguity of entries which are classified as belonging simultaneously to several word classes, such as *authentique* and *lourde* (adjectives and - rather astonishingly - verbs), *plus* (verb and adverb), *entre* (preposition and verb), *chambre, rôle, hausses* and *risques* (both as nouns and verbs)[3]. The last two examples can be eliminated in the grammar as a source of error by a specifying "3rd person" in every verb form.

The third local grammar
The unreliability of the second grammar led me to want to investigate the use of verbs in the four texts, both as to what types of verbs were used and as to which tenses among present, future and conditional were the most frequent in the different text types. The following simple grammar was put to work here:

Local grammar 3:
(<V:P3>+<V:F>+>V:C>)

The examples extracted clearly showed that the multi-ambiguity of lexical forms does lead - when no syntactic filter can be applied - to inefficient and almost useless results (more than 50% errors). Some of the more peculiar examples of lexical forms considered as verb forms by the dictionary, such as

---

[3] See also the multiple tagging of *modèles* in ex. 1.

article (*articler?*), *brute, doctrine, indice, quittance* (*quittancer?*), *référence, tolérance* (*tolérancer?*), and *victime* (*victimer?*) underline that the aim of the LADL dictionaries to be complete and exhaustive clashes with the more precise demand of an automatic text analyzer to be restrictive and realistic as to frequent and active words and word forms. A possible solution to this problem might be to set up a "local dictionary" for the text(s) in question, a local dictionary where rare and improbable forms are filtered out, *before* the "local grammar" is put to work.

Inefficient as it was in extracting only correct verb forms, the third local grammar turned out to be useful. For it demonstrated that the use of the future and conditional was more frequent in the law text than in the other text types, just as the use of modal verbs (*pouvoir* and *devoir* especially) was more frequent in the law text. I will return to this fact later when commenting upon the specific and non-specific readings of indNP.

The fourth local grammar
A first glance at the legal texts revealed considerable syntactic complexity, with a plethora of attributives, insertions, subordinates, nonfinite clauses, etc. This constitutes another complicating factor for automatic analysis, as the local grammar has to take into account this complexity in the only way allowed by the program, namely by introducing a number of "empty categories" ("E") or arbitrary words ("MOT"). The program however rejects an analysis (by the message "trop d'ambiguïtés"), when the number of "E" or "MOT" excedes a certain limit, in the order of 5 or 6. This is far from being sufficient to transcend the syntactic complexity of legal texts.

In order to get an idea of the syntactic complexity of the four legal texts, I set up a fourth grammar designed to recognize occurrences of verbs in nonfinite forms: the infinitive (W), present participle (G) and past participle (K):

Local grammar 4:
(<V:W>+<V:G>+<V:K>)

This grammar rendered a fairly reliable result with only a few ambiguities such as *devant, maintenant, cependant, plus*. It served to permit a second small statistical summary, illustrating the frequency of nonfinite verb forms as compared to finite verb forms (forms which are not verbs in the actual context have been filtered out manually):

Table 2.

	Finite Vb	Nonfinite Vb
Law text (ca 1800 words)	26typ, 53tok	89typ, 115tok
Judgement (ca 310 words)	3typ, 6tok	22typ, 23tok
Text book (ca 1200 words)	35typ, 58tok	75typ, 106tok
Article (ca 1890 words)	46typ, 66tok	118typ, 138tok

The table shows how highly frequent nonfinite verb forms are in the legal texts as compared to finite verb forms.

The fifth local grammar
Encouraged by this apparently reliable result, a fifth local grammar was designed, aiming at elucidating the syntactic function of indNP *following* nonfinite verb forms:

Local grammar 5:
(<V:W>+<V:G>)/(<MOT>+<E>)/(<MOT>+<E>)/(<MOT>+-<E>)/(<MOT>+<E>)/(<MOT>+<E>)/(un+une)/<MOT>/<-MOT>/<MOT>

This grammar, correctly, found examples such as the following:

> être une oeuvre de Nicolas
> attribuant dans tel ou tel cas une importance particulière à
> conférer aux usagers un droit de stationnement
> réaffirmer une solution désormais bien

The sixth local grammar
As local grammar 5 with nonfinite verbs had given a first hint as to the syntactic function of indNP, I tried to run the same syntactic search, but with finite verbs. Accordingly, the following local grammar was set up:

Local grammar 6:
(<V:P3>+<V:I>+<V:S>+<V:J>+<V:F>+<V:C>)/(<MOT>+-<E>)/(<MOT>+<E>)/(<MOT>+<E>)/(<MOT>+<E>)/(<-MOT>+<E>)/(un+une)

This grammar worked, but only partly, as it yielded some strange examples, again due to the intrinsic ambiguities of the dictionary. The following list gives an idea of the results (the words in parentheses have been added manually, as the present grammar was too "short" to extract the noun):

> *a place pour un (essentiel subjectif)*

> *constituent bien une (question juridique)*
> *est un (simple droit de stationnement)*
> *est une (mesure de police)*
> *existait un (lien contractuel)*
> *fait que réaffirmer une (solution désormais bien établie)*
> *gère le parc de stationnement dans un (aéroport)*
> *glissa spontanément dans une (équipe)*
> *jointe à une (clause)*
> *justifie une (fois encore)*
> *poussaient un (véhicule)*
> *véhicules dans un (parc fermé)*
> *victime qui avait apporté une (aide bénévole)*

What was worse here was that this grammar revealed that not only can the LADL programs not transcend "full stop", but they cannot go across a comma either. Manually, I found examples like the following which were not registered by the grammar though they corresponded to the string being sought:

> *On sait que, pour une jurisprudence aujourd'hui bien établie, ...*
> *il en existe, en particulier, une autre*

As a result of using these six search procedures, it can be said that the LADL programs function well as to extracting lexical word-forms and lexical combinations, but that, when it comes to syntax which can only be simulated via word ordering, and especially when it comes to strings where verbs are involved, the LADL programs are not - in their present state - suited for automatic text analysis.

Conclusion

It has nevertheless been possible, by using the LADL dictionaries and programs, to arrive at some interesting conclusions concerning the use of indNP in the present legal texttypes, and consequently to formulate some answers to the five questions asked in the beginning of my paper.

A first set of conclusions concerns the syntactic functioning of indNP in texts. IndNP appears to assume all kinds of syntactic roles:

> subject: *une société hôtelière réclamait*
> real subject: *il existait un lien contractuel*
> object: *ouvrent une simple faculté*
> indirect object: *a été rendu à un grand nombre d'échanges*
> agent: *est réglementé par une loi*
> prepositional phrase: *a place pour un essentiel subjectif*
> and predicative position: *être un droit commun impératif*

The grammars can extract examples like these, but owing to the many errors and to the inherent limitations to searching only between full stops and commas, the grammars cannot, unfortunately, be used to carry out statistics as to which syntactic function(s) is (are) most frequently assumed by indNP.

The second set of conclusions deals with the semantics of the verbs that are constructed with indNP. One group of verbs seems to be semantically close to predicate constructions, such as for instance:

> *constituer un/une N*
> *présenter comme un/une N,*

constructions that do not then introduce new discourse referents.

Another group of verbs, on the other hand, contains a semantic feature "new" which is perfectly compatible with the introduction of new discourse referents. For instance verbs as the following:

> *ouvrir (une simple faculté)*
> *attribuer (une importance particulière à quelqu'un)*
> *entraîner (une réduction)*
> *donner (un droit à quelqu'un)*
> *offrir (un reglementation)*

Another way to consider this type of construction would be to count them as frozen expressions, the verb being a support verb:

> *entraîner une réduction = réduire*
> *avoir une influence sur = influer sur, influencer*

In this latter case, the number of truly discourse referent-introducing indNP would be even more reduced.

A last set of conclusions concerns the last three questions put above: the distribution of indNP for abstract versus concrete nouns and with a specific versus a non-specific interpretation; and, finally, the relationship between the above-mentioned types of indNP and text types[4].

The first grammar revealed that the legal article studied contained a very high number of indNP as compared to the other text types (about three times as many as the law text and the text book). A closer reading of the indNP in the legal article shows that they refer far more frequently to **concrete nouns**[5] than the indNP in any of the other text types. Actually, the law text contained

---

[4] See text samples in the appendix.

[5] Examples are *un album de photos, un aéroport, un bar, un hôtel*, etc.

only one concrete noun, the text book none at all, whereas the only two indNP in the legal judgement both referred to concrete nouns, namely the object of the proceeding. Furthermore, it can be stated that concrete nouns lend themselves more often to a specific reading than do abstract nouns, and they seem to be more easily maintained in the discourse world by anaphoric expressions, such as personal and demonstrative pronouns. Abstract nouns seem more prone to lexical repetition, either with a definite or with an indefinite determiner.

If we relate this to the use of tense and mood in the four texts, the following rather interesting distribution of concrete/abstract, specific/non-specific, present/future, and +/- modal verbs, can be verified:

	JUDGMENT TEXT	ARTICLE	TEXTBOOK	LAW TEXT
past	concrete N specific	concrete N specific		
present		abstract N non-spec.	abstract N non-spec.	
future				abstract N non-spec. modal vb

The judgment refers with its only indNP in a non-predicative position, *un tableau*, to the origin in the history of the litigation. The legal article seems to fall into two parts: the "stories" of actual cases, which are narrated in the past tense and contain many concrete nouns referring to specific persons, places, objects, etc. But the legal article also contains discussions of these cases, discussions which are carried out in the present tense, with a high frequency of abstract nouns (such as *un arrêt, un litige, un accord, une question, une solution*, etc.), that lend themselves to non-specific readings.

The textbook sample, which contains few indNP as a whole, mostly in predicative position (of the definition type "X is a Y") and no concrete nouns whatsoever, is dominated by the present tense, a sort of "all-time present" and by a non-specific reading of the indNP. And, finally, the law-text is characterized by the use of future tense and modal verbs such as *pouvoir* and *devoir*, which - according to certain semantic theories about specificity[6] - is an inherent feature of the non-specific readings of indNP.

---

[6] See for instance Banys, 1983.

The aspects I have enumerated rather sketchily in my conclusion, and which are based on the empirical pilot study carried out here using the LADL electronic dictionaries, merit a deeper-going theoretical study and perspective. This, I believe, should go in a semantic-textual direction, taking into account on the one hand the semantics of indNP as discussed by Emmon Bach in *Nouns and Noun Phrases* (1968) and on the other hand their textual role as presented by Lauri Karttunen in *Discourse Referents* (1976) or their role in the building up of discourse universes as argued by Gilles Fauconnier in *Espaces Mentaux* (1984).

References

Bach, E. (1968) 'Nouns and Noun Phrases', in: E. Bach and R.T.Harms (eds): *Universals in Linguistic Theory*, N.Y..

Banys, W. (1983) *L'Ambiguité référentielle des phrases à descriptions indéfinies en français*. Université de Katowice.

Dyrberg, G. et al. (1991) *Oprettelse af Fagsproglige Tekstkorpora. Engelsk-Fransk-Dansk aftaleret*. ARK 60, Copenhagen Business School.

Fauconnier, G. (1984) *Espaces Mentaux*, Paris.

Karttunen, L. (1976) 'Discourse Referents', in: J.D. McCawley (ed): *Notes from the Linguistic Underground. Syntax and Semantics*, Vol. 7. Academic Press, London.

Courtois, Bl. (1990) et M. Silberztein (éds): *Dictionnaires électroniques du français*. Langue Française 87.

Appendix

The legal article

...

[65] Le second arrêt a été rendu par la Chambre sociale, le 21 juillet
[66] 1986 (Bull. civ. V, n° 421, p. 320). <Un salarié s>'était rendu sur
[67] les ordres de son employeur dans <un garage pour faire> réviser son
[68] camion. Parvenu là, il se glissa spontanément dans <une équipe
[69] d>'employés qui poussaient <un véhicule pour l>'amener sur <une
[70] fosse>, et se blessa en tombant dans cette dernière, au moment
[71] même où la manoeuvre venait de se terminer. La Cour de cassation
[72] approuve les juges du fond d'avoir retenu la responsabilité
[73] contractuelle du garagiste: 'l'arrêt attaqué relève que les
[74] ouvriers des Etablissements Craeye (le garagiste), éprouvant des
[75] difficultés à pousser <un camion> jusqu'au-dessus d'<une fosse>,
[76] avaient agréé l'offre spontanée que leur avait faite M. Garnier
[77] de se joindre à leurs efforts; peu important que l'accident ne se
[78] soit pas produit pendant le déplacement même du véhicule mais au
[79] moment même où cette manoeuvre venait de se terminer, la cour
[80] d'appel était fondée à en déduire qu'il était survenu au cours de

[81] l'exécution d'<une convention d>'assistance conclue dans l'intérêt
[82] des Etablissements Craeye et qui, à défaut de circonstances
[83] particulières, n'impliquait nullement que la victime qui avait
[84] apporté <une aide bénévole fût> devenue le préposé occasionnel de
[85] cette société'.

The judgement

...

[16] LA COUR; - Sur le premier moyen: - Vu l'art. 1110 c.civ.; -
[17] Attendu que, les époux Saint-Arroman ayant chargé Rheims,
[18] commissaire-priseur, de la vente d'<un tableau attribué par
[19] l>'expert Lebel 'l'Ecole des Carrache', la Réunion des musées
[20] nationaux a exercé son droit de préemption, puis a présenté le
[21] tableau comme <une oeuvre originale> de Nicolas Poussin; que les
[22] époux Saint-Arroman ayant demandé la nullité de la vente pour
[23] erreur sur la qualité substantielle de la chose vendue, la cour
[24] d'appel, estimant qu'il n'était pas prouvé que le tableau
[25] litigieux fût <une oeuvre authentique de Poussin>, et qu'ainsi
[26] l'erreur alléguée n'était pas établie, a débouté les époux Saint
[27] Arroman de leur demande; qu'en statuant ainsi, sans
[28] rechercher si, au moment de la vente, le consentement des
[29] vendeurs n'avait pas été vicié par leur conviction erronée que le
[30] tableau ne pouvait pas être <une oeuvre de Nicolas Poussin>, la
[31] cour d'appel (Paris, 2 fvr. 1976) n'a pas donné de base légale à
[32] sa décision; ...

The law text

...

[128] Art. 11. - Tout locataire ou occupant de bonne foi peut exiger la
[129] remise d'<une quittance ou d>'<un reçu à l>'occasion d'<un règlement effectué par> lui.
(...)
[141] De plus, au cours du premier semestre, les hausses de tarifs
[142] découlant de l'alinéa 1er du présent article ne pourront
[143] entraîner <une hausse de plus> de 6 p. 100 par rapport aux tarifs
[144] en vigueur le 31 décembre 1977.
...

The text book

...

[64] 3° Ultérieurement, l'État a été plus loin dans la mesure où il a
[65] voulu diriger toute l'économie de la nation. Or chaque contrat
[66] individuel a <une influence sur cette économie>. D'où la
[67] promulgation de nombreux textes qui tendent à 'diriger' les

[68] contrats, c'est-à-dire non plus à offrir aux parties, comme le
[69] faisait le code civil, <une réglementation à caractère>
[70] interprétatif, s'appliquant à défaut de volonté contraire, mais à
[71] enfermer au contraire cette volonté dans <un cadre> rigide,
[72] impératif, construit en fonction des intérêts généraux.

Lexicon and Terminology

Bodil Nistrup Madsen
Copenhagen Business School

Terminology forms an essential part of Language for Special Purposes (LSP). When developing systems for automatic analysis of LSPtexts it is therefore necessary to include investigations in terminology.

In the present paper, I should like to address some problems relevant to the FAGFLADE project, which is being carried out in the Department of Computational Linguistics, at the Copenhagen Business School. The aim of the FAGFLADE project is to develop theories and methods for automatic interpretation of LSP texts. FAGFLADE is short for *Danish fagsproglig grænseflade* (LSP interface) and interface here means knowledge acquisition interface, i.e. a program which can transfer the information contained in a natural language text into knowledge representations in a knowledge base, cf. Hansen and Vikner (1989). The FAGFLADE project has as its basis the text of the Danish Companies Act (*Lov om aktieselskaber*). It is not the ambition of the project group to construct a complete text interpretation system, but rather to investigate problems in the domain of syntactic and semantic analysis, parsing strategies, knowledge representation, dictionary databases and terminological analysis. The terminological problems to be solved are primarily related to the lexicon and the knowledge base:

- which types of terminological information are necessary in the lexicon and the knowledge base?
- which types of terminological information - if any - can be extracted automatically?
- is it possible to use the information stored in the lexicon for knowledge acquisition as well as for interpretation of user's questions to the knowledge base and generation of answers?
- how is the terminological information to be formalized in the lexicon and the knowledge base?

One way of getting started with these complex problems is to consider the questions which users may put to the knowledge base and the answers which should be given, as well as to investigate whether the text chosen for the project, the Danish Companies Act, contains the necessary information, and whether this information can be correctly identified and analyzed, not by a program but by a human being, e.g. a terminologist. Of special interest are

Steen Jansen et al (eds): Computational Approaches to Text Understanding,
© Museum Tusculanum Press, Copenhagen 1992

terminological problems such as the identification of multi-word terms, synonyms, definitions and conceptual relations.

1. Types of user's questions
User's questions to a knowledge base containing information on the regulations of the Danish Companies Act may be of the following kinds:

    1. theoretical   2. concrete

1.1 questions concerning definitions	1.2 questions concerning rules	2.1 questions concerning validity	2.2 questions concerning calculations
(answers: definitions)	(answers: rules)	(answers: yes/no)	(answers: numbers)

Below I shall give some examples of user's questions and along with these try to demonstrate whether it is possible to identify the necessary information in the law.

The translations of the cited sections are taken from the English translation of the Danish Companies Act (1984). In a few cases the translation has been slightly changed.

1.1 Questions concerning definitions
When discussing definitions one must always have the intended user group in mind. Different users need different levels of specialization. Laymen need definitions with a low level of specialization, whereas subject specialists need definitions with a high level of specialization. If the knowledge base should be designed to meet the needs of different user groups, it may be necessary to offer several definitions of the same concept with different levels of specialization.

    Examples:

    (1)   Hvad forstår man ved fondsaktieemission?
               (What is meant by bonus share issue?)

    (2)   Hvad forstår man ved aktieklasse?
               (What is meant by class of shares?)

    (3)   Hvad er forskellen på præferenceaktier og B-aktier?
               (What is the difference between preference shares and   shares with limited voting rights?)

1.1.1 Re (1) Definition of *fondsaktieemission*

Information on *fondsaktieemission* (bonus share issue) is found in sections 29, 39, 110 and 111 of the Danish Companies Act.

> § 29. Beslutning om forhøjelse af aktiekapitalen ved tegning af nye aktier eller ved overførsel af selskabets reserver til aktiekapital (fondsaktieemission) træffes af generalforsamlingen, jfr. dog § 37, med den stemmeflerhed, der kræves til vedtægtsændring.
> Stk. 2. Forslag om kapitalforhøjelse skal fremlægges til eftersyn for aktionærerne og tilsendes disse efter de herom i § 73, stk. 4, indeholdte regler samt fremlægges på generalforsamlingen.
> (29.-(1) A resolution to increase the share capital by subscription of new shares or by transfer of a company's reserves to the share capital (bonus share issue) shall be passed by the company in general meeting, cf. however, section 37 of this Act, by the majority of votes required for alteration of the articles of association.
> (2) A proposed resolution for increase of the capital shall be open for inspection by the shareholders and shall be sent to the shareholders in accordance with the rules to that effect contained in section 73(4) of this Act and shall be submitted to the company in general meeting.)

From section 29 we learn that *fondsaktieemission* (bonus share issue) is one method for *forhøjelse af aktiekapitalen* (increase of the share capital) by means of *overførsel af selskabets reserver til aktiekapital* (transfer of company's reserves to the share capital) as opposed to the other method *forhøjelse af aktiekapitalen ved tegning af nye aktier* (increase of the share capital by subscription of new shares). Thus we get the elements for an analytic definition with the definiens containing the genus proximum and the characteristic feature which distinguishes this concept from the co-ordinate concept.

> § 39. Fondsaktieemission kan ske ved overførsel til aktiekapitalen af sådanne beløb, som efter § 110 kan udbetales som udbytte, eller af beløb fremkommet ved opskrivning af aktiver eller ved overførsel fra den lovpligtige reservefond eller den særlige fond, der er omhandlet i § 111, stk. 2.
> (39.-(1) The issue of bonus shares may be effected by transfer to the share capital of such amounts as may be paid in the form of dividend under section 110 of this Act, or of amounts resulting from writing up of assets, or by transfer from the statutory reserve fund, or the special fund referred to in section 111(2) of this Act.

From section 39 we get a further specification of the reserves or amounts which may be transferred to the share capital:

- sådanne beløb som efter § 110 kan udbetales som udbytte
  (such amounts as may be paid in the form of dividend under section 110 of this Act)
- beløb fremkommet ved opskrivning af aktiver
  (amounts resulting from writing up of assets)
- ved overførsel fra den lovpligtige resevefond
  (by transfer from the statutory reserve fond)
- ved overførsel fra den særlige fond der er omhandlet i § 111, stk.2.
  (by transfer from the special fund referred to in section 111 (2) of this Act.)

In section 110 the amounts which may be paid in the form of dividend are further specified.

§ 110. Som udbytte kan kun uddeles årets resultat (årets overskud) i henhold til det godkendte årsregnskab for sidste regnskabsår, overført overskud fra tidligere år og andre reserver, der ikke er bundne ifølge lov eller selskabets vedtægter, efter fradrag dels af udækket underskud, dels af beløb, der i henhold til lov eller vedtægterne skal henlægges til den lovpligtige reservefond eller andre formål. Udgør den lovpligtige reservefond ikke en tiendedel af aktiekapitalen, må udbyttet højst fastsættes til seks pct. af den indbetalte aktiekapital.
(110.-(1) No dividend shall be paid otherwise than out of the result for the year (profits for the year) according to the adopted annual accounts for the immediately preceding financial year, profits brought forward from previous years, and other reserves which are not tied-up reserves according to the law or to the articles of association of the company after deduction, partly of uncovered losses, partly of amounts which, pursuant to the law or to the articles of association of the company, shall be transferred to the statutory reserve fund or set aside for other purposes. Where the statutory reserve fund does not amount to one tenth of the share capital, dividend shall be payable at a rate not exceeding six per cent. on the paid-up share capital.)

Section 111 gives information on transfers to the statutory reserve fund and the special fund.

§ 111. Af den del af årets overskud, der ikke medgår til dækning af muligt underskud fra tidligere år, skal mindst ti pct. overføres til den lovpligtige reservefond, indtil denne udgør ti pct. af aktiekapitalen. Henlæggelse skal derefter ske med mindst fem pct., indtil fonden udgør en fjerdededel af aktiekapitalen. Vedtægterne kan foreskrive pligt til større henlæggelse.
  Stk. 2. Til en særlig fond skal henlægges beløb, som selskabet ved aktietegning modtager for aktierne ud over disses pålydende med fradrag af omkostninger ved selskabets stiftelse eller aktiekapitalens forhøjelse,

samt beløb, som selskabet har modtaget ved salg af aktier i henhold til § 40.

Stk. 3. Den lovpligtige reservefond og den særlig fond, der er omhandlet i stk. 2, kan bruges til:
1. dækning af underskud, der ikke dækkes af det beløb, der kan anvendes til udbytte,
2. fondsaktieemission, medmindre selskabet har et udækket underskud,
3. under de i § 46 angivne betingelser til andre formål.

(111.-(1) Not less than ten per cent. of the portion of the profits for the year which is not applied to cover any possible losses from previous years shall be transferred to the statutory reserve fund until such funds constitute ten per cent. of the share capital.

Thereafter transfers shall be made to the extent of not less than five per cent. until the fund constitutes one fourth of the share capital. The articles of association of the company may lay down a duty to make transfers in excess thereof.

(2) Money received by the company in connection with the subscription for shares in excess of the nominal value of such shares shall, after deduction of expenses in connection with the formation of the company or increase of the share capital, be allocated to a special fund together with amounts received by the company through the sale of shares pursuant to section 40 of this Act.

(3) The statutory reserve fund and the special fund referred to in subsection (2) of this section may be applied to:
1) the covering of losses which are not covered by the amount which may be paid out as dividend;
2) the issue of bonus shares, provided always that the company does not have any uncovered losses;
3) other purposes, subject to the conditions laid down in section 46 of this Act.)

Thus section 39 gives further specialization to the information in section 29, and sections 110 and 111 further specialize the information in section 39. The same levels of specification may be used when deciding upon which information may be relevant to different user groups.

In fact this example is not typical of the Danish Companies Act, as it normally contains no information which can be used in definitions or only incomplete information.

1.1.2 Re (2) Definition of *aktieklasse*

In the case of *aktieklasse* (class of shares) the law does not give such detailed information as in the above example.

§ 17. Alle aktier har lige ret i selskabet. Vedtægterne kan dog bestemme, at der skal være forskellige aktieklasser. I så fald skal vedtægterne angive forskellighederne mellem aktieklasserne, størrelsen af disse og eventuelle

begrænsninger i fortegningsretten til nye aktier ved forhøjelse af aktiekapitalen, jfr. § 30, stk. 2.
(17. All shares shall have equal rights in a company. The articles of association may, however, provide for different classes of shares. In that case the articles shall specify the differences between the classes of shares, the amount of such shares, and any restrictions on the right of pre-emption to subscription for new shares in the case of increase of the share capital, cf. section 30(2) of this Act.

From section 17 we learn that there may be different classes of shares and that *vedtægterne skal angive forskellighederne mellem aktieklasserne* (the articles of association shall specify the difference), but we do not get any information on the differences. However, section 17 refers to section 30 subsection 2.

§ 30. Ved enhver forhøjelse af aktiekapitalen har aktionærerne ret til forholdsmæssig tegning af de nye aktier.
Stk. 2. Er der flere aktieklasser, for hvilke stemmeretten eller retten til udbytte eller udlodning af selskabets midler er forskellig, kan der i vedtægterne tillægges aktionærerne i disse klasser forlods ret til at tegne aktier inden for deres egen klasse. Aktionærerne i de øvrige klasser kan i så fald først herefter udøve deres fortegningsret i henhold til stk. 1.
(30.-(1) The shareholders shall have a right to proportional subscription of the new shares in the case of any increase of share capital.
(2) If there are several classes of shares with different voting rights or rights to dividend or distribution of company assets, the articles of association may give the shareholders in such classes a right of pre-emption to subscribe shares within their own class. If that is the case the shareholders in the other classes may only thereafter exercise their pre-emption right under subsection (1) of this section.

From this section we get the information that shares may differ with respect to *stemmeret* (voting rights) and *ret til udbytte eller udlodning af selskabets midler* (rights to dividend or distribution of company assets).
Section 67 gives the rules for increasing the voting value of certain shares.

§ 67. Enhver aktie skal give stemmeret. Vedtægterne kan bestemme, at visse aktiers stemmeværdi forøges, dog ikke ud over ti gange stemmeværdien af nogen anden aktie af samme størrelse.
(67.-(1) All shares shall carry voting rights. The articles of association may provide that the voting value carried by certain shares be increased, provided always that no share shall carry more than ten times the voting value carried by any other share of the same denomination.)

1.1.3 Re (3) Differences between *præferenceaktie* and *B-aktie*

From the above sections on classes of shares we get neither the definitions nor the actual terms denoting the different types of shares. Ideally it should be possible to get an overview of the relationships between shares such as the one given below:

Bold characters signify the different criteria according to which shares may be subdivided into groups.

AKTIETYPER
TYPES OF SHARES

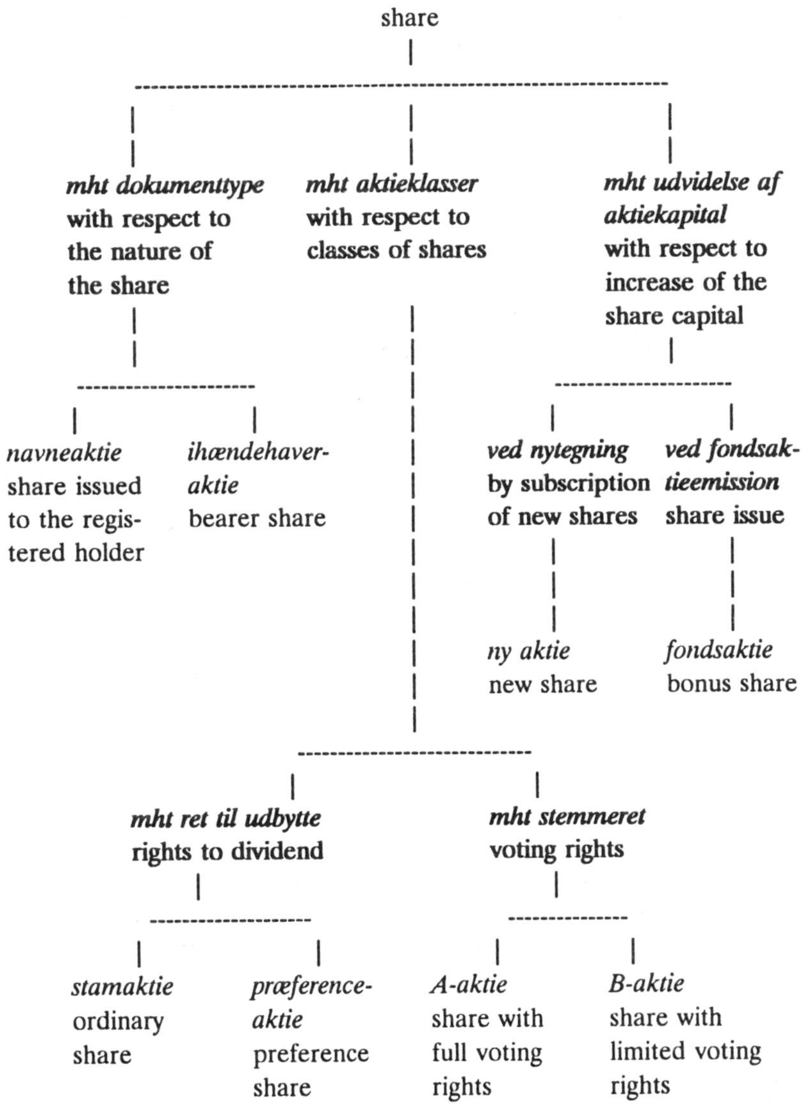

```
                                    share
                                      |
        ---------------------------------------------------------------
        |                             |                               |
  mht dokumenttype            mht aktieklasser              mht udvidelse af
  with respect to             with respect to               aktiekapital
  the nature of               classes of shares             with respect to
  the share                                                 increase of the
                                                            share capital
        |                             |                               |
   -----------                        |                     -----------------
   |         |                        |                     |               |
navneaktie  ihændehaver-              |              ved nytegning    ved fondsak-
share issued aktie                    |              by subscription  tieemission
to the regis- bearer share            |              of new shares    share issue
tered holder                          |                     |               |
                                      |                  ny aktie      fondsaktie
                                      |                  new share     bonus share
                    ------------------------------
                    |                            |
             mht ret til udbytte          mht stemmeret
             rights to dividend           voting rights
                    |                            |
              -----------                   -----------
              |         |                   |         |
          stamaktie  præference-         A-aktie    B-aktie
          ordinary   aktie              share with  share with
          share      preference         full voting limited voting
                     share              rights      rights
```

The shareholder of a *præferenceaktie* (preference share) has increased rights to dividend or distribution of company assets. The shareholder of an *A-aktie* (share with full voting rights) has increased voting rights compared to a shareholder of a *B-aktie* (share with limited voting rights).

According to some descriptions of share types, *A-aktie* (share with full voting rights) is considered to be synonymous with *stamaktie* (ordinary share). This is probably due to the fact that more than one criterion may apply to one share (e.g. a *B-aktie* will often at the same time be a *præferenceaktie*). Due to the lack of specificity of the law mis-communications may arise.

Since the relationships between concepts contribute to the definition of each concept it may be worthwhile investigating other kinds of relationships than the generic, the part-whole, and the temporal relationships which are normally used in terminology work. Among those other relationships are: causal, genetic, material, instrumental, functional and transmission relationships.

1.2 Questions concerning rules

Examples:

(4) Hvilke betingelser skal være opfyldt for at der kan udbetales udbytte?
(What are the conditions for paying a dividend?)

(5) Hvilke beløb kan anvendes til forhøjelse af aktiekapitalen ved fondsaktieemission?
(What amounts may be used for the increase of the share capital by a bonus share issue?)

(6) Hvilke betingelser skal være opfyldt for at der kan ske fondsaktieemission ved overførsel fra den lovpligtige reservefond?
(What requirements should be met in order to allow bonus share issue by a transfer from the statutory reserve fund?)

(7) Hvornår kan der udstedes friaktier?
(When is it possible to make a scrip issue?)

The rules may be deduced from sections 29, 39, 110 and 111 (see above). The main function of a law is to give rules; thus it is not surprising that it is easier to find this kind of information than to find proper definitions of concepts.

The problem of identifying synonyms is not especially related to the questions concerning rules. However, the above examples may be used to illustrate this problem.

Both the text interpreter and the question interpreter must be able to realize that the following expressions of the law are synonymous:

forhøjelse af aktiekapitalen (§ 29)
(increase of share capital)

kapitalforhøjelse (§ 29)
(increase of the capital)

aktiekapitalens forhøjelse (§ 111)
(share capital's increase)

kapitaludvidelse (in the index of the law)
(the raising of additional capital)

Section 111 contains two synonymous expressions:

skal overføres til
(shall be transferred to)

skal henlægges til
(shall be allocated to)

Question (7) illustrates the problem of missing information since the term *friaktie* (share issued by a scrip issue) which is a synonym to *fondsaktie* (bonus share) is not used at all in the law.

2.1 Questions concerning validity

Examples:

(8) På generalforsamlingen er repræsenteret 3/5 af den stemmeberettigede aktiekapital (= 3 mio kr.). Ved en afstemning om forhøjelse af aktiekapitalen ved fondsaktieemission afgives i alt 150 stemmer. Heraf er 105, repræsenterende i alt 1,5 mio kr. aktiekapital, for en fondaktieemission. Er beslutningen om forhøjelse af aktiekapitalen gyldig?
(In the general meeting members representing three fifths of the share capital (= 3 million kroner) are present. In a vote to increase the share capital by means of a bonus share issue a total of 150 votes are cast. Out of these 105 votes representing 1.5 million of the share capital are in favour of a bonus share issue. Is the resolution to increase the share capital valid?)

(9) ID A/S har en samlet aktiekapital på 5 mio kr. Den lovpligtige reservefond var pr. 1.2.1985 250.000 kr.

Overskuddet for året 1985 udgør 500.000 kr. og der er ikke underskud fra 1984. Firmaet vil gerne udbetale 400.000 i udbytte. Er det lovligt?
(The share capital of the company ID Ltd. amounts to 5 million kroner. As at 1 February 1985 the statutory reserve fund amounts to 250,000 kroner. The profits for the year 1985 amount to 500,000 kroner and there are no uncovered losses from 1984. The company wants to pay a dividend of 400,000 kroner. Is this legal?)

The answer to (8) can be found in section 29 (see above) and section 78:

§ 78. Beslutning om ændring af vedtægterne i andre tilfælde end dem, som er nævnt i §§ 16, 38, 42, 47 og 134e, træffes på generalforsamlingen. Beslutningen er kun gyldig, såfremt den tiltrædes af mindst to tredjedele såvel af de afgivne stemmer som af den på generalforsamlingen repræsenterede stemmeberettigede aktiekapital. Beslutningen skal i øvrigt opfylde de yderligere forskrifter, som vedtægterne måtte indeholde, samt de særlige regler i § 79.
(78. Any resolution for alteration of the articles of association shall, in cases other than those referred to in sections 16, 38, 42, 47, and 134e of this Act, be passed by the company in general meeting. Such resolution shall be valid only if carried by not less than two thirds of the votes cast and by attending members representing two thirds of the share capital carrying voting right. The resolution shall in all other cases comply with any other provisions which might be laid down in the articles of association, and with the special provisions of section 79 of this Act.)

The question in (9) may be answered by using section 110 (see above).

2.2. Questions concerning calculations

Examples:

(10) ID A/S har pr. 1.2.1986 en samlet aktiekapital på 5 mio kr. Den lovpligtige reservefond var pr. 1.2.1985 250.000 kr.
Overskuddet for året 1985 udgør 500.000 kr. Hvor stort et beløb må udbetales som udbytte for 1985?
(As at 1 February 1986 the share capital of the company ID Ltd. amounts to 5 million kroner. As 1 February 1985 the statutory reserve fund amounted to 250,000 kroner. The profits for the year 1985 amount to 500,000 kroner. How much dividend may be paid out for the year 1985?)

(11) Pr. 1.2.1987 udgjorde reservefonden 1 mio kr. Overskuddet for 1987 er på 600.000 kr. Hvor stort et beløb kan anvendes til fondsaktieemission?
(As at 1 February 1987 the statutory reserve fund amounted to 600,000 kroner. How much can be used for a bonus share issue?)

The answers to these questions may be found in sections 110 and 111 respectively (see above).

The answers to both questions concerning validity and calculation are based on the same rules as mentioned in 1.2 above, and it is not surprising that the law contains the information needed. Of course the same problems of identifying synonyms as mentioned above exist in connection with these types of questions.

A similar problem is the identification of the relationships between super-/subordinate concepts. If for example in question (11) the user uses the superordinate concept *forhøjelse af aktiekapital* (increase of share capital) instead of the subordinate concept *fondsaktieemission* (bonus share issue), the answer generator should be able to look up possible rules for different types of increase of share capital and present them to the user. In this case only the rule concerning bonus share issue is relevant. Alternatively the system could ask the user whether the question concerns *tegning af nye aktier* (subscription of new shares) or *fondsaktieemission* (bonus share issue).

2. Conclusions as to the terminological information in the law

The above examples illustrate that the Danish Companies Act does not contain all the terminological information needed for interpreting and answering user's questions:

- It is not possible to find precise definitions of all relevant concepts;
- It is not possible to find current terms;
- Information on the relationships between concepts is imprecise or missing.

3. Formalization of the terminological information

For the time being, the lexicon to which the parser, FAGPARS, has access, is stored as a Prolog database, cf. Hansen and Vikner (1989). However, experiments will be made to store the dictionary data as an ORACLE database.

In the structuring of such a dictionary database the experience from the structuring of terminological data in the terminological database, DAN-TERM, may be useful. For example DANTERM contains for each concept the following information on conceptual relationships:

- system of concepts (SYSTEM),
- position of the concept in the system (POS),
- related concepts eg. super-/subordinate concepts (REL) and
- the type of relationship (e.g. BC-GEN = broader concept, generic relationship).

One advantage of storing the dictionary data in an ORACLE database may be the 'reusability' of the data in that, once entered into ORACLE, it can be extracted in different forms for different purposes.

References

Danish Companies Act (1984). Unauthorized translation of Aktieselskabsloven (1984). Revisionsfirmaet C. Jespersen, GEC Gads Forlag.

Hansen, Steffen Leo and Carl Vikner (1989) *FAGFLADE: The Initial Phase of a Project in Natural Language Interpretation*, LAMBDA 11. Copenhagen Business School.

Lov om aktieselskaber (1986). Lov nr. 370 af 13. juni 1973, jfr. lovbekendtgørelse nr. 483 af 15. november 1985 med lov nr. 317, 318 og 324 af 4. juni 1986 indarbejdet. Schultz Grafisk A/S, København.

Which Rules of Inference Can be Used in Automatic Text Analysis?

Jørgen Olsen and Steen Jansen
University of Copenhagen

1. The text analysis project

The problems of inference that we want to deal with here, are problems that have come up in the *actual* state of a project[1], the purpose of which is to write a program in Prolog for automatic *text analysis*.

The fundamental approach we have adopted can be expressed schematically:

Text -> Question-Answer-Dialogue -> Output

the output is an 'extended text', which includes the sentences of the original text *and* the sentences which are the result of the 'question-answer-dialogue' (as it is in the elementary implementation discussed later in this paper); it can be seen as an updated representation of the discourse universe or of shared knowledge or simply as a new supplementary text.

In contrast to many similar AI projects, the essential feature of this approach is that we draw no distinction between a 'read-time', in which the understanding of text takes place, and a 'question-time', in which the proper understanding is controlled (cf Charniak (1997, 52) and (1985, 11); Lehnert (1978, VIII) and (1983, 16)). We claim that there are good reasons to think that the very act of reading is already a question-answer process, and that this dialogue *produces* understanding; otherwise it would be difficult to explain, among other things, how two readers can come up with quite different understandings (often in the form of different answers to the same or similar questions) about the same text.

In text analysis there seems to be at least two basic strategies: either to find all possible rules that are supposed to be necessary for a complete understanding of the text, or to use a method that deals with the notion of partial information depending on the *purpose* of the actual text analysis. We have chosen the latter method because we work on the assumption that text understanding is based on a dynamic principle, i.e. we use "historical" knowledge, build up and destroy entities of the discourse world during the process of text understanding - and also because our approach is based more on philological principles or traditions concerning text analysis than on

---

[1] CODEXIN (Steen Jansen, Jørgen Olsen and Henrik Prebensen)

psychological theories of memory, language behaviour and acquisition of textual information.

2. The modules in the project of automatic text analysis

In our concept different modules perform different parts of the analysis, and the following reflections should be understood as suggestions as to the kinds of elements that a text grammar must contain, and it is obvious that we, to some extent, use many notions and functions belonging to traditional linguistic areas.

In the following description of our attempt to implement a procedure for an automatic text analysis we will enumerate and discuss the problems we have been able to foresee up to now.

The project, at present, envisages (cf Prebensen (1991)) the construction of

(A)   a *NL module*, which translates both NL questions and text sentences into a semantic representation language; it encompasses

(1)   a *parser*, segmenting input into constituents, using a *lexicon* (lexemes), a *syntaxicon* (syntaxemes or grammatical words) and a *grammar* (set of productions). Output is *a set* of constituents, not a phrase structure. (cf Prebensen (1990, 105))

(2)   a *functional* module determining certain functional categories (*focus, subject, object,...*).

(3)   a *case-grammar* module using output from a. and b., case-frame information attached to the verb and case-rules to generate a case-frame representation of the 'inner structure' of the sentence. (In the implementation illustrated below this module is not used.)

(4)   a *complement-grammar* module placing the inner structure and as much as possible of the residual constituents in an 'outer structure' (*modality, time, place*), thus generating a propositional representation of the sentence. (This module has not yet been constructed.)

(B)   an *Inference module*, comprising

(1)   a *search* module, which in the text database finds sentences matching the question primarily on the basis of verbal information.

(2)   a *unification* module, which (a) unifies question and sentence, both in formal representation, or (b) starts an inference mechanism.

To each module in the NL module corresponds a set of "grammar" rules controlling the parsing, the determination of functions and case roles; they are written in plain text, using few and standard symbols, and are stored in a simple text-file. It is essential to the project that these rules should form an independent part, distinct from the program itself. In this way no prolog programming is involved in writing the rules; different sets of rules can be formulated and changed, depending upon specific purposes, interpreters, contexts and so on, without having to change the program: last but not least, a given set of rules should never be "hidden" in the program, but should be "transparent", open to discussion, possible rejection or revision.

3. Inference and coherence

In automatic text analysis one of the main questions will be if the system in some way is able to "react intelligently" on the basis of its own model of its actual "world", which in our case is the stored text plus some extra stored information. This kind of information is made explicit by inferences in the understanding process.

(1) Skårene fra den knuste rude lå overalt på gaden.
(The pieces from the broken window were spread all over the street)
(2) Den lille dreng stod grædende ved siden af.
(The little boy stood crying close by)

If (1) and (2) appear in this order in a text, the basic assumption will be that there is a connection between the boy and the broken window. An attempt will therefore be made to compute just how this coherence can be established.

Even in apparently quite incoherent entities like:

(3) Peter blev hentet ved toget. Faderen er skorstensfejer.
(Peter was fetched at the train. The father is a chimney sweep)[2]

investigastion has shown that a reader at least tries to establish a connection between 'Peter' and 'the father' as the agent in the action of 'to fetch'. So, when one is saying that a reader of a text tries to ground his understanding on implicit information, he means that the reader starts some mechanisms of understanding that are developed by the acquisition of a given language. In other words the reader uses the inference rules which the text permits and invites the reader to employ.

4. Unification and inference

Our use of inference mechanisms are based on the assumption that one can draw conclusions from the entities of a text and their structure.

---

[2] *the father* is a literal translation of Danish 'fader*en*'. English would not have the *same* source of referential indeterminacy, only one comparable to it.

A further goal of the inference mechanism is to test if already stored information is compatible with or contradictory to the knowledge, which is produced by the actual process of inference. This knowledge is stored in the system, so that it can keep in check, *why* a given information unit is present (and if necessary expand or change it). In this sense *meaning* is generated by unification or by inference, by which different expressions are transferred to the same equivalence classes.

Unification (i.e. a complete match between the language units) alone does not suffice as a tool for automatic analysis of texts, the aim of which is some kind of understanding. We need a system that can 'reason at runtime', i.e. call rules (like the inference rules in PROLOG) during analysis wherever it pays off to shorten the process of searching through facts, often structured as databases. In other words: when the linguistic entities alone can no longer provide the necessary information, we intend to use inference rules. So the task is to derive the meanings from the text entities, not only from the explicit information, attached to the manifest entities in the text (words, phrases), but also from what we have called the implicit information.

5. Types of inference

A. Valency

(4)   Drikker Peter?
       (Does Peter drink?)

(5)   Drikker Peter nu?
       (Does Peter drink now? or Is Peter drinking (now)?)

In (4) one can normally reason that Peter has an alcohol problem, while (5) is more questionable. We need more context in order to decide which inferences can be done on the basis of this text. The examples show that at least two points must be considered. First, we must have information which can tell us that a divalent verb in elliptic use can carry implicit meanings over and above the meaning included in single words. Secondly, all elements must be considered in the analysis, in (5) even the word 'nu', which in traditional valency theory does not belong to the obligatory structure of the verb 'drikke'. Nevertheless such an element plays an important role in *text* analysis: it must therefore be considered if information of this kind should be placed in the verb lexicon or in more general inference rules. Such rules should then state that a combination of a verb plus a temporal unit 'normally' conveys the canonical meaning of the verb, in this case 'drikke' (to drink).

(6)   Peter tog sig af hende af medlidenhed.
       (Peter looked after her out of pity)

In attempting to answer the question 'What did Peter do?' on the basis of a text like (6) we are faced with two preposition phrases and have to make a choice to decide their grammatical values. Here we can derive - from the *position* of the constituent - the information that 'af hende' (her) belongs to the verb's valency structure and consequently add a special kind of information, for instance that 'af hende' has an immediate relation to another constituent: the subject/agent.

B. Anaphoric Resolution

Anaphoric constituents can be resolved by information from features of the verb. In

(7)   Katten så mælken; *den* drak *den*, selv om *den* skilte.
        (The cat saw the milk; it drank it, even if it curdled)

the verb 'drak' (drank) demands an 'animated subject' and a 'liquid object', while 'skilte' (curdled) only demands a 'liquid subject'. So questions like: *Hvad gjorde katten?* (What did the cat do?) and *Hvordan var mælken?* (How was the milk?) can be answered by using the inherent features of the verbs. In

(8)   Peter har ramt Paul med en sten.
        (Peter has hit Paul with a stone)
(9)   *Den* har skadet *ham* en del/*Det* har skadet *ham* en del.
        (It has hurt him a great deal/This has hurt him a great deal)

the case is more sophisticated. We can infer from 'ramt' (hit) that a non-subject has been hurt. When 'den' (it) has been unified with 'sten' (stone), inferencing starts. After a look-up in the lexicon in the entry 'skade' (hurt) (here we find a reference to 'ramme' (to hit)) a proper unification takes place. The inference rule will then as a preference have the direction <away from the subject> by the anaphoric solution from (9) to (8) (i.e. from 'ham' (him) - not to *Peter*, but to *Paul*).

But if a proper unification cannot take place (from 'det' (this) to 'sten' (stone)) then the inference rule has to trigger another directionality: a reference *via* the content of the whole sentence *to* a person mentioned in (8). This kind of inference would probably demand more text than the actual one.

C. Premises and Conclusions

More complicated is the relation between the information in premises and the conclusion.

(10)   Peter går i skole. Peter er flittig.
        (Peter goes to school. Peter is studious)

If we put the question: *Er Peter dygtig?* (Is Peter clever?), is it then possible to conclude from (10) that this is the case? The general problem here is to decide whether the premises contain more, less or the same amount of information as the conclusion.

It seems that in natural languages only the latter is the case, *if* one claims that the premises "command" the conclusion. For 'clever' includes linguistically that one has more *properties* than 'to be studious' and 'to go to school'.

The conclusion can only be based on what can implicitly be the result of an inference rule in the reader's understanding mechanism, and it will not be activated until we put questions like *Arbejder Peter meget i skolen?* (Does Peter work much in school?).

Here can be inferred: *Er Peter flittig i skolen?* (Is Peter studious in school?), and this phrase can be unified with the text. With the question *Er Peter en dygtig elev?* (Is Peter a clever pupil?) there can only be made assumptions by means of "probalistic" reasoning: it may be an implication of the text, but on the other hand this solution might be unacceptable to some readers; in this case the answer is: That cannot be decided on the basis of the text.

6. Toulmin's argument scheme as a tool to manage the search for a proper answer

In experimental projects for setting up and testing different types of inference rules, many have tried to classify rules by superior principles. It is evident that the inference principle per se is unique in linguistic research: we decide what follows from what. But in actual use it has been suggested that it should be possible to distinguish between types of semantic/pragmatic rules in in addition to strictly logical ones, based on *inclusion vs. non-inclusion*. The list of such types is like the following:

> *specifications - causatives - resultatives - motivation - instrument - knowledge propagation - negation* (cf. Schank 1975, 193)

However, these specifications, which were intended as reductions in the rule devices, lead to atomism or to infinite discussions about concrete classifications of information.

Besides, our fundamental approach also implies, especially when we speak about inference, that in general we will adopt a rather classical view on logical relations: we do not try to find substitutes for the traditional ones: conjunction, disjunction, implication and so on, but to solve problems about how to organize the use of such relations, how to make explicit the principles of such an organization and how to decide which are the acceptable propositions (linguistic or formalized) on which these relations should operate.

It seems therefore more reasonable to consider, which argument levels we need and consequently refer to in the analysis, as e.g. Toulmin's argument schemas do.

The management of inference rules can be based on a distinction between several different levels. Such a structuring of rules should primarily depend on how many times or how 'deeply' we have to analyse questions to the text. If e.g. the anaphorical circumstances in examples like (7) are so obviously clear that a single look-up in the lexicon gives an adequate answer, then the analysis can stop here. But if there are obscurities in the text, inferences must be started, i.e. when the proper unification does not work, the inference rules must be invoked.

However, in general it is hard to distinguish between knowledge based on "purely linguistic" rules and rules based on "world knowledge"; for the reasoning in this project is solely bound to linguistic signs.

But in this context it might be possible to use Stephen Toulmin's technique concerning the nature of arguments. Besides, he also discusses variation in the need for involving specific types of arguments. According to Toulmin, a statement (in Toulmin = data) instigates a reader to ask: "*What* can you derive from this statement, and how can you ground it?". In order to answer this question, we can find arguments from domains of other kinds than the text, e.g. rules, principles, inferences. Toulmin names these arguments *general hypothetic statements*. They can function as bridges, leading to an adequate grounding for the data and the conslusions that can be drawn from them.

Transferred to part of our text:

DATA: 'Fire engelske orlogsmænd kræver at visitere Frejas konvoj' (four English warships demand to search the Freja's convoy)

(possible) CONCLUSION: *They want to engage in battle*

SINCE (=warrant): a demand connected with the action *visitere* (to search) implies *enmity*

ON ACCOUNT OF (=backing): *visitere* is codified as an action that can be exercised only by authorities without implying enmity

UNLESS (=qualifier): the context not already in other respects indicates disagreement between the two actants, e.g. enmity, hostility.

This framework is a possible structuralizing of knowledge, based on a normal flow of arguments. The leading idea should be that one could stepwise draw on this hierarchical system for information. The starting point should be determined by heuristic principles.

7. Implementation of an elementary inference module

The actual, elementary implementation takes the following example as input:

The Text:
(11) fregatten Freja kommer 25. juli i Kanalen i kamp med fire engelske orlogsmænd.
(12) de kræver at visitere Frejas konvoj.
(13) efter en tapper kamp må Freja stryge flaget.
(on July 25 in the Channel the frigate Freja engages four English warships.
they demand to search the Freja's convoy.
after a brave fight the Freja is forced to strike its colours.)

The questions:
(14) hvornår kommer Freja i kamp?
(when does the Freja become engaged in battle?)
(15) hvad gør Freja i Kanalen?
(what does the Freja do in the Channel?)
(16) hvem kræver at visitere Frejas konvoj?
(who demands to search the Freja's convoy?)
(17) taber Freja kampen?
(does the Freja lose the battle?)
(18) vinder Freja kampen?
(does the Freja win the battle?)
(19) vinder englænderne kampen?
(do the English win the battle?)

This is obviously an extremely simple example: it is a very short text, slightly simplified in relation to the original; the questions too are very simple: there are no negations nor quantifiers and there are only *who-, where, when-* and *yes/no*-questions. However, we think the example can serve our purpose, which is to try to give an initial idea about the problems of implementation that is to give a "catalogue" with an ordered and clear division of the different problems.

A. Representation of the question.
The representation of the question must enable a search for the "best" sentence in the text and then a comparison between the question and this sentence.

Here we have chosen to form two lists on the basis of the output from the parser and the functional modules in the NL module; the output from these modules is a database containing the constituents forming the question, some of them with functional labels.

The first list is a list consisting of the constituents with their functional labels; in general these are relational (*subject, verbal, object* etc.), except for one case where it is positional (*focus*). This function is specific to Danish: it is the first constituent of the sentence, the second being always the verbal, and it can have any relational function other than verbal. When it is not possible to attach a specific function to the constituent in the functional module, we use the label *remainder* (it will normally be adverbial constituents or prepositional phrases attached to other constituents). To constituents expressing time or place are further attached the labels *time* or *place*.

These elements in the list are ordered in a canonical way corresponding to that of the declarative sentence that is: *subject, verbal, object, remainder*; the elements with the labels *time* and *place* are placed/located at the end of the list.

This list will be used for the comparison between question and sentences in the text.

Question:
(14)   hvornår kommer Freja i kamp?
The question in canonical declarative form:
(a)   ["subject Freja","verbal kommer","remainder i kamp","time focus hvornår"]

The second list in the representation of the question contains the same constituents, but without any label and without the question-word; these are placed in a fixed, but different order: *verbal, subject, focus, object, remainder,* ...; this order reflects the "importance" given, at present, to each element.

This list is used for searching the "best" sentences in the text.

List of search-words/constituents:
(b)   ["kommer","Freja","i kamp"]

B. Search for possible unificanda.

The first module of the inference module is a search module (cf above); it has been introduced in order to avoid parsing *all* the sentences of the text.

The sentences are examined, from the beginning of the text, matching (with a simple string-match) each element in the search-list and the entire, actual sentence. To each sentence is given an index, depending on the *number* of successful matches and the *value* of each match (the first element counts more than the second, the second more than the third and so on); to be successful the entire element in the list (i.e. the entire constituent) must match a part of the sentence (so "Freja" and "i kamp" give successful matches with the first sentence above because it contains "fregatten Freja" and "i kamp", but "med kamp" would not).

Next the sentences which have been examined are ordered according to the index they have received, so the sentence with the highest index, and therefore probably the "best" candidate for an acceptable answer, comes first, next comes the sentence with the second highest index and so on. With the actual question the sentences of the small text are ordered as follows: (11) - (13) - (12).

If there is no match at all, the answer, in the actual implementation, will be no answer, as in the case of the last question:

Question:
(19)   vinder englænderne kampen?
       (do the English win the battle?)
The answer is:
       Måske, men teksten siger ikke noget om dette.
       (Perhaps, but the text says nothing about this.)

With the actual question (14) the result of the search will then be

The "best" sentence for a possible answer:
(11)   fregatten Freja kommer 25. juli i Kanalen i kamp med fire engelske orlogsmænd.
       (on July 25 in the Channel the frigate Freja engages four English warships.)

Only at this point is a formal representation of the sentence produced, following the same principles as with the question; it has this form

The sentence in canonical declarative form:
(c)   ["subject fregatten Freja","verbal kommer","remainder i kamp","remainder med fire engelske orlogsmænd","time remainder 25 juli", "place remainder i Kanalen"]

In order to facilitate the control of the unification that follows, another list is formed in the present implementation; it is the search-list already produced, now supplied with the relevant labels from the question-list:

(d)   ["verbal kommer","subject Freja"," remainder i kamp"]

As we have shown above the answer can be found in two ways: by *unification* or by *inference* in a more reduced sense.

C. *An answer based on premises in the text*: **unification**
Only if the text itself contains the premises for the conclusion, which will be the answer, it will be possible to establish unification that is unification between each constituent in the question and a corresponding constituent in one or more sentences in the text - with the exception of that of the question-word which has to be instantiated with a value from a corresponding constituent in a sentence in the text.

In the present implementation, two constituents can be unified if their functional labels (and *time* or *place* labels if present) are identical, and if the "text-string" of the question-constituent is identical with or part of the "text-string" in the sentence-constituent, e.g. *place remainder i Kanalen* and *place remainder i Kanalen* or *subject Freja* and *subject fregatten Freja*.

The *focus*-label can be unified with any other proper functional label except the *verbal*-label, e.g. *focus* and *object* or *place focus* and *place remainder*.

If the "text-string" in the sentence-constituent is a "referential" word (e.g. a pronoun), the preceeding sentence is examined for a constituent with the same morphologic features (later also semantic features, and other elements, should obviously be taken into account) as the "text-string" in the question-constituent, e.g. *hvem* (16) is unified with *de* (12) which further is compared to (resolved anaphorically with) *fire engelske orlogsmænd* (11); the variable *hvem* can then be instantiated with the value *fire engelske orlogsmænd*.

As the exampels show, the question-word is considered a variable which is instantiated with the text-string, i.e. the value, in a corresponding constituent of the sentence, e.g. *time focus hvornår* with *time remainder 25 juli*.

Notice that the answer contains all the constituents of the question, but not necessarily all those of the sentence.

Later these constraints, and others, should all be expressed in inference rules outside the program.

The whole unification process, between the question-list and the sentence-list ((a) and (c) above), is controlled by the extended search-list (d): the attempts to unify two constituents are carried out in the order determined by this list, i.e. first an attempt with the verbal, next with the subject and so on. If a unification fails, an attempt to use an inference rule (see below) is made, and if this too fails, the whole unification starts anew with the next sentence in the ordered list of sentences.

When a unification succeeds, the corresponding constituent in the question-list is removed; at the end of a successful unification this list contains only the constituent with the question-word, and it is now instantiated with, or replaced by the corresponding constituent in the sentence-list.

Since the question-list is in declarative form, it constitutes the answer to the initial question, when its labels has been removed and it has been transformed to a string:

The answer is:
>   Freja kommer i kamp 25 juli.
>   (the Freja is engaged in battle on July 25.)

The verbs *gøre* and *ske* ("do" and "happen") constitute a special case; we assume here that *hvad gør* ("what does ... do") can be unified with any other verb (plus, in the present implementation, the complements it commands); to distinguish the verb *gøre* from other verbs, a "prefixe" *hv_* is placed in front of the verb when making the list-representation of the question. This "new" text-string will then be unified, or properly instantiated, with the verb in the sentence plus all the constituents between the verbal and the time or place constituent (which has been located at the end of the list).

The entire result of the unification will then be:

Question:
(15)   hvad gør Freja i Kanalen?

Sentence in the text:
(11)   fregatten Freja kommer 25. juli i Kanalen i kamp med fire engelske orlogsmænd.
The question in canonical declarative form :
(a)   ["subject Freja","verbal hv_gør","place remainder i Kanalen"]
List of search-words/constituents:
(b)   ["gør","Freja","i Kanalen"]
The sentence in canonical declarative form :
(c)   ["subject fregatten Freja","verbal kommer","remainder i kamp",- "remainder med fire engelske orlogsmænd","time remainder 25 juli","place remainder i Kanalen"]
Extended search-list:
(d)   ["verbal hv_gør","subject Freja"," place remainder i Kanalen"]

The answer is:
        Freja kommer i kamp med fire engelske orlogsmænd i Kanalen.

D. An answer based on premises in the text and outside the text: *inference*

When one or more sentences in the text are not sufficient to provide an answer that is they do not constitute premises necessary to drawing a conclusion, other premises must be looked for outside the text. This mechanism we name *inference* as opposed to *unification*.

Such premises can be contained in other texts as representations of general, pre-established language-, text- or world-knowledge (such as Schank's scripts, plans, goals etc), i.e. knowledge which should be entirely independent of any individual reader or text. As mentioned above it will be very difficult to determine to what extent such texts can be written.

The premises could also be the result of a man-machine-dialogue, in which the machine, instead of giving an answer as it has done in the preceeding part of the dialogue, "asks" for further information. If the dialogue leads to a successful result, i.e. to an answer, the new premises could be stored (but, in principle, only as reader dependent knowledge to be used by the same reader in subsequent readings, or to be used, in a larger text analysis project, to compare different "reader-profiles"; they can not, without further and detailed discussions, be considered general or common knowledge to be used by anyone).

The present implementation exemplifies a man-machine-dialogue as an inference mechanism (and at present we only try to unify the verbals). We have not yet succeeded implementing a form of Toulmin's argument schema.

If the attempt to unify fails, as it does with

Question:
(17)   taber Freja kampen?
       (does the Freja lose the battle?)

the machine will initiate the following dialogue:

There is no immediate answer, but does the sentence:
       fregatten Freja kommer 25. juli i Kanalen i kamp med fire engelske orlogsmænd.
give the basis for an acceptable answer (y/n)? N
New candidate-sentence is:
       efter en tapper kamp må Freja stryge flaget.
does this sentence give the basis for an acceptable answer (y/n)? Y
More information is needed:
       Are 'taber' and 'må stryge' synonyms? (1)
       Are 'taber' and 'må stryge' antonyms? (2)
       None of the two. (0)
Choose one of the numbers: 0
       Are 'taber' and 'må stryge flaget' synonyms? (1)
       Are 'taber' and 'må stryge flaget' antonyms? (2)
       None of the two. (0)
Choose one of the numbers: 1

Question:
       taber Freja kampen?
The answer is:
       Freja taber kampen.
       (the Freja loses the battle.)

The same sort of dialogue will take place after

Question:
(18)   vinder Freja kampen?
       (does the Freja win the battle?)

where *'vinder'* and *'må stryge flaget'* are antonyms, as a result of the dialogue, so

The answer is:
>Freja vinder ikke kampen.
>(the Freja does not win the battle.)

with the insertion (in the declarative form corresponding to the question) of a negation *ikke*.

Beside the answer, another result of the dialogue is the updating of a database; in the present case two facts, or equivalence-lists are stored, namely:

>[["taber"],["syn"],["må","stryge","flaget"]]
>[["vinder"],["ant"],["må","stryge","flaget"]]

One can easily envisage other relations than "syn(onym)" and "ant(onym)", and perhaps even more complex; such a database can later on be used as a representation of acquired knowledge, either general or reader-dependent.

E. Updating the shared knowledge (or the discourse universe).

After each successful unification or inference (of the entire question and sentence), the answer to the question is, in the present implementation, added to the text; so now the text has, with the questions given above, the following form:

New text:
>Freja kommer i kamp med fire engelske orlogsmænd i Kanalen.
>Freja kommer i kamp 25 juli.
>fregatten Freja kommer 25. juli i Kanalen i kamp med fire engelske orlogsmænd.
>fire engelske orlogsmænd kræver at visitere Frejas konvoj.
>de kræver at visitere Frejas konvoj.
>Freja taber kampen.
>Freja vinder ikke kampen.
>efter en tapper kamp må Freja stryge flaget.
>
>(the Freja engages four English warships in the Channel.
>the Freja is engaged in battle on July 25.
>on July 25 in the Channel the frigate Freja engages four English warships.
>four English warships demand to search the Freja's convoy.
>they demand to search the Freja's convoy.
>the Freja loses the battle.
>the Freja does not win the battle.
>after a brave fight the Freja is forced to strike its colours.)

This new text can be seen as a representation of knowledge now shared by the reader and the text('s author (fictional or real)). One result of this adding new information to the original text is that if the reader now asks 'does the Freja lose the battle?' then the answer will be immediate, without the dialogue shown above, and it will be simply 'yes' (and the same goes for the question 'does the Freja win the battle?'; the answer is 'no'). This is due to the fact that now the initial search for an adequate sentence will be made in the new text and not only in the original one.

8. Conclusions

In the project we are looking for rules of inference that can give access to the understanding of connections expressed either ex- or implicitly. Thereby we could bring forward a meaning that satisfies our demands: something means something, if it corresponds to the syntactic or semantic role of an expression in a text. For instance: *'Peter* IS *a person who can act'* or 'between *search* and *convoy* there IS a relation', which we can verify through other texts.

We certainly have not yet solved the problem of inferencing - and we did not pretend to do so; however we think that we have established a basis for future investigation into the still very complex problem, and we hope that this basis will allow us to distinguish more clearly between the different subproblems and to try to solve them one by one.

References

Charniak (1977): 'Organization and Inference in a Frame-like system of Common Sense Knowledge', in: Schank & Nash-Webber: *Theoretical Issues in NLP*. Cambr. Mass.

Charniak and McDermott (1985): *Introduction to AI*. Reading Mass.

Lehnert (1978): *The Process of Question Answering*. Hillsdale, New Jersey.

Lehnert et al (1983): 'BORIS, An Experiment In-Depth Language Understanding', in: *Artificial Intelligence* 20,1.

Prebensen (1990): 'Interpretation in Dynamic Text Understanding', in: *Papers from The Second Nordic Conference on Text Comprehension in Man and Machine*. Stockholm.

Prebensen (1991): 'DELAL', in: *Papers for a seminar on CODEXUS*. DATA HUMANA 8, Institute of Informatics, University of Copenhagen.

Schank (1975): *Conceptual Information Processing*. Amsterdam-Oxford.

Schank and Abelson (1977): *Scripts, Plans, Goals and Understanding*. Hillsdale, New Jersey.

Toulmin (1969): *The Uses of Argument*. Cambridge.

A Formal Approach to Dynamic Text Interpretation

Henrik Prebensen
University of Copenhagen

ANTIPHRASE:
POUR FAIRE UN POEME DADAISTE
Prenez un journal
Prenez des ciseaux
Choisissez dans ce journal un article ayant la longueur que vous
    comptez donner à votre poème.
Découpez l'article
Découpez ensuite avec soin chacun des mots qui forment cet article
    et mettez-les dans un sac.
Agitez doucement.
Sortez ensuite chaque coupure l'une après l'autre dans l'ordre où
    elles ont quitté le sac.
Copiez consciencieusement.
Le poème vous ressemblera.
Et vous voilà 'un ecrivain infiniment original et d'une sensibilité char-
    mante, encore qu'incomprise du vulgaire'.
(Tristan Tzara, *Sept Manifestes Dada*, 1924)[1]

0. Introduction

This text is a reflexion on formalization of text interpretion as practiced in philology as well as in literary and historical criticism. The ultimate goal is computerization.[2]

Using previous formalization is sound methodology, a kind of *stepwise refinement* before programming.

---

[1] TO WRITE A DADAIST POEM. - Take a newspaper/ Take some scissors/ Choose in the newspaper an article of the length you want to give to your poem./ Cut out the article/ Next clip cautiously each of the words from the article and put it into a bag./ Shake gently./ Then sort each cutting one after the other in the order in which they leave the bag./ Copy with diligence./ The poem will be like yourself./ And you has now become 'an infinitely original poet possessing a charming sensibility, though as yet unintelligible to the vulgar'./ (Tristan Tzara, *Seven Dada Manifestos*, 1924)

[2] This work is pursued in collaboration with Steen Jansen and Jørgen Olsen in our common project, CODEXIN, (*Computational Dynamic Text Interpretation*).

Steen Jansen et al (eds): Computational Approaches to Text Understanding,
© Museum Tusculanum Press, Copenhagen 1992

The goal is not to imitate processes or representations located in the mind of a Platonic reader. The idea is to draw conclusions about text meaning using rational methods which make up the technique of the humanistic scholar in text analysis. The scope is theory and practice in the human sciences, not cognition.

1. Text interpretation as a humanistic practice

Some important assumptions underlying text and discourse interpretation in the Humanities are made clear in the following four quotations, two from newspaper articles in literary criticism, two from University textbooks on literary and historical method. They illustrate essential features of the ordinary text interpretation practitioner's view:

(1) Among Hans Christian Andersen's *Fairy Tales*, the *Shadow* is certainly the text which he himself prized most highly, a masterpiece with a rich potential of interpretations and depths. That a piece of world literature is deep and has many layers of interpretation, does not mean, however, that any reading of it makes sense. (Bettina Heltberg, *Politiken*, 92.1.23, 2,6)

Taking the word *reading* to denote the result of a text interpretation, one could say that (1) views the relationship between a text and its readings as one-many. A text does not determine its readings. It only constrains them. To put matters extensionally: a text selects a (possibly infinite) subset of readings from the (infinite) set of all possible readings. The task of text analysis is to prove the validity of a specific reading, presumably chosen for its relevance in some other respect.

(2) There are a couple of things readers must know in order to enjoy (Henry) Miller. Some warnings and some recommandations. Now and then, reading him is boring.
   This is one of Miller's good qualities (...) He is no modern author for female readers. He is an oldfashioned author for female readers, an author for intimacy. You have to skip pages now and then (even among the audacious ones, because you don't feel like reading them, not this time, not now). You control your own reading (...) just read ahead. This is the clue. Begin where you want, at the page you want. (Mogens Rukov, *Read Miller! Information*, 92.1.25, 2)

According to (2) *readings* do not necessarily result from a process that starts from the first word in the text and proceeds in nice order without omissions to the last. Readings may differ in the choice of what they incorporate.

(3) it (...) is nonsensical to pretend examining what the text itself says (...) The text only gives replies to questions, and if an inquiry is to serve a scientific, sound purpose, the questions of the scholar must be related to an (...) intersubjectively communicable theory which is falsifiable on the basis of data that can be identified (Arne Schnack 1982, 61)

On (3), a *reading* is the outcome of a dialectic and constructive process. Information units (i-units for short) are actively extracted from the text to serve as building blocks in the reading. An explicitly stated theory constitutes the touchstone for the admissibility of i-units into the reading.

(4) Knowledge is not representation, it is produced in reply to questions that originate in curiosity: what is this? what is true? (...) The conditions for insight is that a challenge forces itself upon the historian provoking him to queries. But his active role is often neglected, because people fix their attention on results. (...) historical knowledge, as other knowledge, should not (...) be understood as a kind of vision, but as complicated structures of questions and answers. (...) Only then do we recognize that insight is produced in a qualitative leap from a question to an answer (...) both embedded in a comprehensive, hierarchic structure of inquiry, i.e. a heuristic endeavour (Carsten Thorborg 1977, 50-51).

(4) brings into focus a dynamic concept of *reading* as a growing tree with a 'query-driven' top down structure where a top query provokes cascading subqueries at lower and lower levels down to terminals. A 'text' may even be a corpus of texts. Readings may be used in ways which are not straightforwardly related to the hypothetical intentions of their authors. In skilled understanding, the ability to distinguish what is true on textual evidence from what one may deduce under certain assumptions is crucial.

Most experiments in automatic text understanding inadequately take texts as having one specific meaning or meaning structure. The task of a program is to generate meaning as a formal representation of 'what the text means'.

Practice in the human sciences takes a reading to be a structured object constrained by a text or text corpus. It is constructed dialectically by an agent on (theoretical) assumptions. It can be discussed and criticized on rational grounds.

2. An example: The murder of King Erik V

The murder of King Erik V of Denmark is an enigmatic historical event. We only have a few fragmentary texts to inform us about it. This small text corpus therefore has offered a fine ground for creative text interpretation.

(5)   Erik V, nicknamed *Clipping* because of his frequent devaluations by 'clipping' silver coins, was the victim of a nocturnal murder on November 22nd 1286, in the small village of Finderup, where during a hunting expedition, he slept in a barn alone with Rane Jonsen, his 'camerarius'.

Four years earlier, in 1282, an opposition of nobles headed by marshal Stig Andersen Hvide, had forced upon the King a constitution instituting the annual convocation of a 'Parlamentum'. They had also dislodged the King's leading minister, the 'dapifer' (royal carver) Peder Nielsen Hoseøl. In 1285, the King crushed his troublesome kinsman, Duke Valdemar of Slesvig, whom six months in prison persuaded to swear eternal fidelity.

At Whitsunday 1287, six months after the murder, the Parlament met in Nyborg. Valdemar of Slesvig had been appointed tutelar to the murdered King's 12 year old son, Erik VI Menved. He and Peder Nielsen Hoseøl, back on stage, accused the leaders of the former oposition. A sentence confiscated their property and proscribed them. This started a 20 year feud where the proscribed obtained overt and active support from the Norwegian King. Only Arvid Bendsen, an armiger far below the rest in social rank, was excluded from this protection.

Sparse texts throw feeble glimpses of light on the events. A few contemporary chronicles describe the event, all in similar terms. They do not name the guilty. They allude to 'men whom the King had loved most' and mention his 56 wounds, 'all but one above the belt'.

The sentence, which is now lost, was produces as testimony before the Papal Court in Rome in 1296, during a process against the Archbishop Jens Grand, accused of treason because of alleged connivance with the proscribed. The Archbishop's advocate stigmatizes the sentence as political. His client knows how and why the King was murdered, but cannot reveal the scandalous truth yet. There also exist letters from the Norwegian King proclaiming the sentence political.

A 17th century historian (Arild Huitfelt) quotes a copy of the sentence, now lost, in which Arvid Bendsen is said to have 'with his own hand attended this heinous murder'.

Between the murder and the trial, Rumelant, a famous German minnesinger who worked for the Danish court, wrote a poem which is a piece of propaganda . It describes the crime in the same terms as the chronicles. But, interestingly, it warns the Danish people against the murderers, who plan to seize power and to plead not guilty, sheltering behind old Danish law (which admits proof of innocence on the oath of twelwe men of good reputation). 'This shall not happen', the poet exclaims. The poem hints at political machinations in connection with the trial.

A flood of ballads on the murder inundates late medieval literature. They explain the murder as a 'crime passionel' or 'drama of revenge'. The lascivious King offends the marshal's wife while he fights for the King. The marshal washes off the offence with blood.

The historian's 10.000 $ question now of course is: *Who murdered King Erik?*

All historians agree that the marshal is innocent. He has no motive. He and his group had been in power since 1282. The murder ruined their situation. They could only suffer from a politically unstable situation.

Historians also agree that, from November 1286 until the trial at Whitsun 1287, a palace revolution to the advantage of Duke Valdemar and the 'dapifer' Peder took place.

It is generally believed that Arvid Bendsen must have been actively involved.

For the rest, serious works on Danish history leave the question unanswered. No compelling evidence identifies the instigators of the murder. Off the record, however, in articles, broadcasts, debates, some historians stick their neck out. A plausible candidate is *Duke Valdemar*. Presented as a deduction, this conclusion takes the Roman *cui bono* principle as a premiss: *He who benefits, instigated*. Duke Valdemar benefited, beyond any doubt. He got rid of his suzerain, became a member of the regency of the child King, all obligations forced upon him in 1286 were revoked. His fief was increased. He was the winner.

The example demonstrates text interpretation in practice. The crucial challenge: *who murdered King Erik V?* If the corpus does not give a simple answer, a search starts provoking new questions which sort out subcorpora of relevant passages from which pieces of information are extracted. If, however, the corpus is too thin to yield a conclusion, we are the free to 'guess'. Guessing, technically, takes additional assumptions to support deductions. The fewer and the simpler these assumptions, the more satisfactory the conclusions (*Occam's razor*).

3. Prolegomenon to a formalization

I use the following notation:

(6)   upper-case Greek letters denote texts or text corpora,
      upper-case Roman letters denote sets of sentences,
      lower-case Greek letters denote sentences or predicates,
      lower-case Roman letters denote arguments

Standard symbols are used for logical connectives, commas for logical conjunction. '$\top$' and '$\bot$' mean *true* and *false*.

The formalism employs standard concepts for systems of logical deduction, LD:

(7) $LD =_{Def} <L, \vdash>$

where   L is a language, not necessarily formalized, but rich enough syntactically and semantically for us to assign sentences to semantic equivalence classes of any fineness of grain we want;
$\vdash$ denotes a relation of deduction; consequences may be a single sentence or a sequence of sentences or a set of sentences.

If seen *dynamically*, '$\Gamma \vdash \phi$' denotes a move taking the system from a state in which the set, Γ, of premisses is available, into a new state where ϕ is also avail-able. We choose '$\vdash$' to be governed by rules of a natural deduction version of intuitionistic logic. In intuitionistic logic, there is no rule of *indirect proof*: $\neg\phi,....,\perp \vdash \phi$). Therefore *tertium non datur* ($\phi \vee \neg\phi$) is not valid, either. The truth value of ϕ may be unknown until a proof of ϕ has been found. Heyting algebras, not Boolean algebra, provide a semantics for L.

Logical truths (tautologies, theorems) are deduced from an empty set of premisses:

(8) ϕ is a *logical truth* iff $\vdash \phi$

For a *text interpretation system*, TI, we use a notation similar to '$\vdash$' in (7)

(9) $\Gamma \Vdash \phi$

'$\Vdash$' means that the reading ϕ (a single i-unit) can be derived from the text Γ in the system.

Tautological readings derive from the empty text:

(10) ϕ is a *tautological* reading iff $\Vdash \phi$

There is an obvious relationship between *deduction* and *derivation of a reading*. Somehow, the validity of a reading has to be *proved*. It may be conjectured that the relationship is a relation of *inclusion*. We therefore want to find a mapping from texts and readings onto sets to subsume '$\Vdash$' and '$\vdash$' under one rule, i.e.

(11)   if $\Gamma \Vdash \phi$ then $\Gamma \vdash \phi$

4. Texts and Sets

A text is a set of sentences with a relation of order, whereas sets of premisses are unordered. If the same sentence appears twice in a set, the two occurrences count as one member. In a text, order is semantically significant. Two occurrences of the same sentence would have different contexts and hence represent different meanings, that is constitute two different items.

If we do as Tristan Tsara and put all sentences from a text into a bag, context-dependent information is lost. The set will not represent the text.

Context-dependent information in a text is as in conversation. Participants build a *universe of discourse* which they share. Information from it is presupposed in subsequent discourse, e.g. for anaphoric resolution. Presupposed information also appears as *common knowledge*. Finally, linear order is often exploited in *iconic representation*, and presupposed e.g for temporal indications.

Practice in §§ 1-2 showed that text analysis need not respect order. Readers may 'swoop down upon' a passage or read discontinuously. Historians use whole text corpora selectively. Interpretation does not follow a linear order imposed by the text.

At a low level, text interpretation works on minimal information units (i-units). At this level, text Γ is treated as a set of independent i-units. If a sentence contains context dependent unknowns, the context is skimmed for resolvants. Presuppositions relying on context will be spelled out. A text segment (sentence) like

(12)a. The admiral ignores his commanding officer's orders, putting the telescope to his blind eye

might - somewhat pedantically - be turned into

(12)b. As event e_i, Admiral Nelson, in the battle of Copenhagen, on the morning of April 2, at moment m_j, ignores the orders of Admiral Parker, Admiral Nelson's commanding officer. As event e_j, Admiral Nelson, in the battle of Copenhagen, on the morning of April 2, at moment m_j, puts Admiral Nelson's telescope to Admiral Nelson's blind eye.

Thus a linearly ordered text, Γ, is turned into an unordered set, Γ, of sentences, explicitating all implicit information related to order.

We express this in a *principle of text-set congruency*

(13) Given a text, Γ, Γ can always be mapped onto an unordered set of sentences, C, without loss of information. C is called a *congruent set with respect to* Γ

(13) does not claim the *uniqueness* of C. The concept of congruency rests on *loss of information*. This implies a comparative measure of information. Quantity or degree is not an objective property of information. We pigeonhole our concepts into different semantic grids - and grids of varying degrees of coarseness - according to our specific purposes. No system of representation is rich enough to capture all imaginable information that can be extracted from a text.

As a consequence of the principle of text-set congruency, we may now replace Γ with C in (9), so that

(9)a. if $\Gamma \Vdash \phi$ then $C \Vdash \phi$ (by (13))

i.e. if reading ϕ derives from text Γ, it derives from a congruent set C.

The principle of text congruency guarantees the mapping we are looking for. Notice that instead of C, we most often only need consider a subset of C, namely the i-units that are required to derive ϕ, i.e. the congruency mapping may be partial.

5. Readings and Texts

We now turn to the concept of *reading*, ϕ. What kind of entity is ϕ? We have discussed it as a single sentence ϕ. But we may use Tarski's principle of universality:

(14) Wenn man überhaupt über irgend etwas sinnvoll sprechen kann, so kann man darüber in der Umgangssprache sprechen[3]

We may therefore take a reading to be itself a text, Δ. By the principle of congruency any reading can be represented as a set of sentences.

(9)b. if $\Gamma \Vdash \Delta$ then $C \Vdash D$ (by (13) and (14))

If reading Δ derives from text Γ, then congruent set D derives from congruent set C.

Readings are described as dialogues in §§ 1-2. The querying interpreter extracts answers from the text, e.g.

(15) - How did King Erik V die?
 - King Erik V was murdered.
 - Where?

---

[3] Tarski (1935), p. 278. Translation in Tarski (1955), p. 154: if we can speak meaningfully about anything at all, we can also speak about it in colloquial language.

- At Finderup, in a barn.
- Why in a barn?
- On a hunting expedition, he had sought shelter for the night in the barn.
- When was he murdered?
- The night before St Cecilia's day, November 22nd, 1286.
- Who murdered King Erik?
- He was murdered by an armiger, Arvid Bendsen, who is said to have 'with his own hand attended this heinous murder'.
- Was he judged?
- He was judged together with a group of noblemen headed by marshal Stig Andersen.
- Did they participate?
- They do not seem to have participated.. They are all reported to have been two or three days' journey away, except Rane Jonsen, the 'camerarius'.
- Did they instigate the murder?
- We are not told who instigated the murder.
- Assuming that the murderer is always the person who benefits most from the crime, who instigated the murder?
- Assuming that the murderer is always the person who benefits most from the crime, Duke Valdemar of Slesvig is the murderer.

If we eliminate the questions, we obtain the following text:

(16)   King Erik V was murdered. At Finderup, in a barn. On a hunting expedition, he had sought shelter for the night in the barn. The night before St Cecilia's day, November 22nd, 1286. He was murdered by an armiger, Arvid Bendsen, who is said to have 'with his own hand attended this heinous murder'. He was judged together with a group of noblemen headed by marshal Stig Andersen. They do not seem to have participated. They are all reported to have been two or three days' journey away, except Rane Jonsen, the 'camerarius'. We are not told who instigated the murder. Assuming that the murderer is always the person who benefits most from the crime, Duke Valdemar of Slesvig is the murderer.

Texts like (15) or (16) are query driven readings. The strategy of questioning controls the internal structure and order of the reading.

6. Readings and Logical Deductions

All information in (15) and (16) are logical deductions from Γ. The rules of deduction used are not very sophisticated. Stated somewhat informally, they are

(17) 0. If $\phi \vdash \psi$ then $\vdash \phi \rightarrow \psi$
     1. If $\phi \in \Gamma$ then $\Gamma \vdash \phi$
     2. If $\Gamma \vdash \phi$ and $\Gamma \vdash \neg\phi$ then $\Gamma \vdash \bot$
     3. If $\phi a \in \Gamma$ and $a = b$ then $\Gamma, a = b \vdash \phi b$
     4. If $\phi \in \Gamma$ and $\phi \rightarrow \psi$ then $\Gamma, \phi \rightarrow \psi \vdash \psi$
     5. If $\phi \notin \Gamma$ then $\Gamma \vdash \phi \vee \neg\phi$

Rule 0 falls under the *deduction theorem*. It states the relationship between deduction, '$\vdash$', and implication, '$\rightarrow$', so that a proof can be used in new deductions.

Rule 1 says that what a text states consistently is a fact with respect to readings. Arvid Bendsen *is* a murderer if the text says so. To refute it we have to use external assumptions, i.e. assumptions not belonging to the text.

According to rule 2, contradictions invalidate a text. It is important to have methods for identifying contradictions. It is also important to have a methodological rules for cases where texts in a corpus are contradictory.

Rule 3 is the rule of substitution. It says that if two individual entities, a and b, are known to be identical, then the sentence ϕa may be substituted by the sentence ϕb. Substitution is done as unification.

4 is modus ponens. In both 3 and 4 the second conjunct, $a = b$ or $\phi \rightarrow \psi$, may be external assumptions, whereas its first member, a or ϕ, should be in Γ. The *cui bono* rule was an external assumption triggering the conclusion about the role of Duke Valdemar in the murder of King Erik. External assumptions must be stated explicitly.

5 states that in the absence of information, no conclusion is permitted (remember that $\phi \vee \neg\phi$ is neither true nor false in intuitionistic logic).

Logical deduction seems to be able to capture the way in which texts constrain readings. It is certainly not too restrictive. A case where a reading can be justified without being a logical consequence of Γ in the above sense is difficult to imagine.

Logical deduction does not seem too weak, either. Can something be a consequence of Γ, but not enter in any reading?

It seems reasonable to assert that any reading is a logical consequence of its texts or of the text and assumptions made by the interpreting agent i.e.

(18) $\Gamma \Vdash \Delta$ iff $C \vdash D$ (cf. (9)b)

If a reading Δ derives from a text Γ, then a set D congruent with Δ is deducible from a set C congruent with Γ. Or, in other terms, Δ is a reading of Γ if we can find a logical proof of D from C.

7. Computerization

(18) is the end point to this outline-formalization of text-interpretative practice in the human sciences. Can (18) also serve as a starting point for a computerization of this practice?

One might think that a text interpretation system should proceed stepwise from Γ' (a text) to a unique formal representation, Γ, then from Γ via rules of deduction to a formal representation of a reading, ϕ, and finally from ϕ to the reading ϕ'.

In practice, however, as we have seen, text interpretation is initiated by *challenges* which trigger cascades of sub-queries. A text interpretation system therefore should perform as a question-answering information system with the text as a data or knowledge base (see 14). The investigator makes a query. The system translates it using grammars and dictionaries, performs a search for information satisfying the query and returns an answer. A sequence of answers constitutes a reading.

We may distinguish three levels : 1. operational, 2. tactical and 3. strategic. Operational and tactical procedures should be amenable to computerization. They belong to the methodological sphere of *heuristics* and *justification*. Strategic problems belong to the sphere of *invention* and *critique*. They are hardly open to deterministic approaches.

At the operational level, the most difficult problem is natural language (NL) processing. Queries and text segments in NL must be translated into a formal representation to which rules of logical deduction apply. Inferred information must be returned in NL form. Sentences and phrases must have semantic representations, so that units of information of identical content but different form can be unified. There must also be made provision for discourse universes in connection with dialogues.

At the tactical level, we meet problems of choice of appropriate rules of deduction for a specific derivation, and of the search for relevant premisses in a text to meet a query. Unification and meaning postulates on relations of inclusion between lexical items (concepts) seem to be a solution. Of course, there are a subtle, and often controversial distinctions to be made between special strategical assumptions ('world knowledge') backing up a specific reading, and general meaning relations between words. Every day life is full of discussions muddling up word meaning and questions of substance: *What is murder? Is this murder?*

Strategy is mainly concerned with control structures or plans for producing readings. A sequence of queries, making up a reading, i.e. pursuing a specific goal, cannot be set up on operational and tactical information alone. The user is responsible for the overall meaningfulness of his investigation.

Strategic information raises important, but difficult problems. (1) Text coherence. Do texts contain sufficient information on their own internal organization to uncontroversially establish a 'canonical reading', possibly intended by the author, e.g. 'a plot' or 'a theme'? We do not think that texts are self-contained. They only constrain readings, i.e. coherence is not a unique property of a text. (2) Can we set up a universal 'reading model' or at least 'reading models relative to cultural and educational background' which, together with information from the text, impose canonical readings? We will return to this problem below. (3) Are there computational models for producing readings? Whether general reading models exist or not, is it possible to write 'programs' in which a sequence of queries controls an automatic production of a reasonable reading of an arbitrary text? If this should become possible, we have powerful tools for processing text, e.g. that generate summaries or extract 'meta-textual' information on say **main characters, argument**, etc. Until now, attempts in this direction have not been applicable outside the range of artificial and very simple-minded texts.

Anyway, whether strategic problems will admit of automatic solutions, i.e. programs producing 'canonical readings' in a general manner, or not, feasibility depends largely on progress in NL processing, i.e. the possibility of translating expressions into a formalism which permits extensive search and logical deductions.

8. Alternative approaches to text understanding

There are two main trends in computational text understanding.[4] The first is 'text linguistic', which is interested in text coherence and discourse structure.[5] The second, within AI, is interested in modelling a reader's understanding of texts, especially stories, using conceptual representations.[6]

The text linguistic approach focuses on features belonging to rhetoric, *viz.* segmentation of texts and organization of segments in accordance with a plan. It studies text organization on text internal data, as a formal grammar parses sentences and attributes structures to these sentences.

This kind of discourse analysis necessarily proceeds on two levels. First at sentence level where processing produces a representation of how a sentence contributes to the meaning of the segment it belongs to. Boundaries between segments are determined using adverbials, verb typology, focus, determiners, anaphors and tense. The 'textual category' of each sentence is also determined in this process.

---

[4] A good description in Smith (1991), p 378-433.

[5] E.g. Grosz and Sidner (1985). Jerry R. Hobbs (1985).

[6] E.g. Schank and Abelson (1977), Lehnert et al (1983).

The upper level may use a context-free discourse grammar with rules such as:

(19)   STORY → SETTING + EPISODE*
       SETTING → STATE | STATE + EPISODE
       EPISODE → EVENT | EVENT + EPISODE*
       (...)[7]

Terminals are sentences in accordance with the category they were assigned to at sentence level. Sentences correspond to words in a sentence grammar.

This analysis is narrow in its scope. Its purpose is to determine a *unique* and *complete* discourse structure representing ideal linguistic and 'rhetoric' competence of an abstract reader. This structure is a kind of 'canonical reading', but it contains only technical, 'meta-textual' information, which an unsophisticated reader may use in understanding discourse, but which is not in itself 'meaningful', cf. native speakers and grammatical sentence structure.

Next, it is doubtful that context free rules of sentence grammar and discourse grammar alone determine coherence and structure of texts. Grosz and Sidner consider discourse structure to be a composite of three interacting components, a linguistic structure (generated by sentence and discourse grammar), an intentional structure and an attentional state. Intentional structure presupposes the identification of a single purpose (among many possible purposes of a discourse) as the *foundational* intention. It is not clear, however, on which information this intention can be determined. Attentional state represents a reduced discourse universe, containing active entities, relations and intentions. It is organized as a stack and memorizes what may be referred to in the immediately subsequent discourse. Stacks work well for the short range, e.g. anaphor resolution, and for recursive embedding. When an element has been popped off a stack, it is unrecoverable. So we face the same problem with discontinuity in discourse structure as in sentence structure.

The story understanding approach is definitely computational. To mimic understanding, it uses scripts, plans, frames or similar conceptual schemes which store stereotyped knowledge about actions or events. When a text is processed, a conceptual scheme is selected, which permits the system to fill in gaps, complete partial information, ascertain hypothetical presuppositions. The text understanding program generates a unique and complete meaning representation of the text, which is an image of what was understood, i.e. a kind of reading. In a second turn, this representation may be used as a database to answer questions to the text. The focus in some of these projects is the study of dynamic memory in cognitive processes or planning within AI.

---

[7] E.g. Rumelhart (1975).

Strange inferences crop up in some cases. E.g. the information that *John went to a restaurant* may trigger a restaurant 'script', which postulates that *John was hungry*, no matter whether there is any question of hunger or not. From a logical point of view, scripts and their counterparts function as (hidden) assumptions added to a text database and used in deductions when no premises can be found in the text. According to the standards of textual criticism, an interpreter should as a minimum distinguish what is in the text from what is not. Nothing forbids conclusions based on your own assumptions, if they are stated explicitly. This means that conceptual schemes should be written in full text and added to the text under investigation to form a corpus of explicit rules or meaning postulates: *If a person goes to a restaurant, he is hungry.*

Both approaches work with readings *uniquely determined* by the text. This idea is incompatible with the views in this article. However, if such readings can be computed by a system, they can also be computed by a dynamic text interpretation system based on the formalism presented here.

It might be objected that *dynamic text interpretation* in our sense is not the same as *text understanding*. Understanding, or even misunderstanding, is always specific. So a representation thereof must be *unique*. The answer to this is that a specific understanding of a text as of anything else is determined by a number of choices, making up a *strategy of interpretation*. If one can design a strategic plan for a specific reading, a dynamic text interpretation system can read the plan as a text and use it as a set of assumptions determining the meaning of the object text uniquely. Programs which are so tightly tied to a specific strategy that only one type of readings can be produced and only from a narrow set of text types are simply too limited to qualify as interesting approaches to text understanding.

9. Conclusion

The formal approach to dynamic text interpretation investigated here relies on query-driven derivation of readings. A reading is only *constrained* by the text, but becomes determined by a strategy of interpretation. This is the standard of text interpretation practiced in the human sciences.

A text (or text corpus) is formally a set of information units into which queries are made. A reading is the information extracted and organized according to the strategy. Extraction of information is based on intuitionistic logical deduction.

At the operational level, the production of a reading presupposes grammatical and discourse oriented techniques of natural language processing, search processes based on informational content rather than form, and, finally, unification.

EXIT
>de chapitre en chapitre
>avançons toujours

page après page
changeons de paysage
et ainsi avançant
nous voici vers la fin
ça y est
(Tristan Tzara, *40 chansons et déchansons*, inédits)[8]

References

Grosz, Barbara and Candace L. Sidner (1985) *The Structure of Discourse Structure*, CSLI Report 85-39.

Hobbs, Jerry R. (1985) *On the Coherence and Structure of Discourse*, CLSI Report 85-37.

Lehnert, W. et al (1983) 'BORIS, An Experiment in In-Depth Language Understanding', in: *Artificial Intelligence* 20,1.

Rumelhart D. E. (1975) 'Notes on a Schema for Stories', in: Bobrow & Collins, (eds): *Representation and Understanding*. New York-San Francisco-London.

Schank, R. C. and R.P. Abelson (1977) *Scripts, Plans, Goals and Understanding*. Hillsdale, New Jersey.

Schnack, Arne (1982) *Textanalyse og teori*. Copenhagen.

Smith, George W.(1991) *Computers and Human Language*. New York-Oxford.

Tarski (1935) 'Der Wahrheitsbegriff in den formalisierten Sprachen' in *Studia Philosophica* I.

Tarski (1955) *Logic, Semantics, Metamathematics*, Oxford.

Thorborg, Carsten (1977) *Arbejdspapirer til historisk metode* (Working Papers in Historical Method), 2. ed., vol. 2. Copenhagen.

Tzara, Tristan (1952) *Poètes d'Aujourd'hui* 32, ed. René Lacôte & Georges Haldas, Paris.

---

[8] from chapter to chapter/ let us make our way still/ from page to page/ through changing landscapes/ going on like this/ lo and behold! we come/ to the end/ that was it (Tristan Tzara, *40 Songs and Missongs*, unpublished) from Tzara (1952).

Dynamic Text Comprehension

Torben Thrane
University of Copenhagen

Information processing systems

The human capacity to understand texts in natural language (NL) is one of the phenomena to be explained on the assumption that we (also) are information processing systems. There are three levels at which any such system must be understood and properly characterized (Marr 1982, 25):

- a level of computational theory, which specifies what the goal of the computation is, why it is appropriate, and what the logic of the strategy is by which it can be carried out;
- a level of representation and algorithms, which specifies how this computation can be implemented; in particular, what the representation for the input and output is, and what the algorithm for the transformation is;
- a level of (physical) implementation, which specifies how the representation and algorithm can be implemented.

The scientific goal, for Marr, is to provide a computationally viable characterization of human vision. The ultimate goal, for me, is to provide a computationally viable characterization of the human capacity for understanding texts in natural language. In both cases, what is involved is an account of the processes by which the human conceptual apparatus picks out and manipulates information from sensory data.

However, I do not believe that the explanations will run parallel for long, if at all, although ultimately they will lead to comparable - or even identical (cf. Jackendoff 1987) - results: the creation of one or more mental representations, which may or may not fit (portions of) the world. But that the processes are distinct - and *categorially* distinct - appears from the simple fact that, although we can all *see* a printed page of Chinese, we cannot necessarily *understand* it. Although seeing a printed page is a necessary condition for understanding it, it is not a sufficient condition. For the mental representations created on the basis of visual input will, by default, have inclination of fit (Thrane 1992) towards the portion of the world that gave rise to the representation, whereas those created on the basis of textual input, although *seen*, will have default inclination of fit to situations *represented* by the input, and they need not be portions of the world at all. This is because texts are concrete manifestations of (sequences of) NL sentences. Text understanding

Steen Jansen et al (eds): Computational Approaches to Text Understanding,
© Museum Tusculanum Press, Copenhagen 1992

is a special case of NL understanding, so an account of text understanding will largely, but not exclusively, be equivalent to an account of NL understanding. For this reason I shall be somewhat lax in my use of the terms 'text understanding/comprehension' and 'NL understanding/comprehension' where nothing hangs on the distinction.

This paper will address some issues pertaining to the first two levels in Marr's hierarchy, concentrating on the nature of the computations and representations involved in the overall process of understanding.

Representation, computation, and explicitation of information

Information processing is a matter of computation, and can, as such, be seen as a function from representations to representations. Representations contain information.

If NL understanding is an instance of information processing, then some form of NL representation is required for the computational processes involved. The most widespread format for NL representation, other than texts, is the formal rules proposed by linguistic theory, which provide representations of the structural properties of the language generated by those rules.

Choice of representation, however, has consequences for computation. A representation is said to *make information explicit* to a process to the extent that it makes that information available to the process without the requirement of further computations. For example, one often quoted reason why the ancient Romans were not doing so hot in mathematics, is that the Roman numeral system is a poor representation of numbers *for mathematical purposes.*

This ties in with Marr's first level, which speaks of the *goal* of computation. The main objective of (Thrane 1992) was to develop one line of argument against the virtually standard view that still more finegrained language *description* will eventually lead to language *understanding.* Here is another.

- Formal linguistic representations have been developed and refined with respect to the number and nature of the computations that can be applied to NL input strings and their derivates. These have brought us noticeably further in (automated) language description.
- Despite this development no noticeable advance in (automated) NL understanding has been forthcoming.
- A major reason for this is that the tacit goal of computations on NL input has been to test the descriptive adequacy of representations of NL structure, and that therefore the information made explicit by representations needed by these computations has been descriptively, rather than interpretively, relevant.

In support of these claims I mention just three wellknown points of linguistic debate with a bearing on the issue:

1. The case of syntactic functions

According to the standard theory, PS-rules like S → NP VP make explicit three items of information:

- categorial membership (labelling)
- linear order among constituents
- dominance relations among constituents

Other items of information, however, can be inferred, eg. information concerning the syntactic functions of constituents. The failure to make this particular item of information explicit prompted developments like Relational Grammar, and to a certain extent Arc Pair Grammar and LFG. On the other hand, insistence on making information concerning linear order explicit prompted, among other things, the development of GPSG. But the main point is that the debates around such issues were debates about *descriptive* adequacy and generality. GPSG may or may not be descriptively more rigorous than the standard theory and its extensions, but it is not a theory whose rules reveal information of a different *kind*, even despite its development of semantic interpretation rules to run parallel with the syntax.

2. The case of computational innovation

The standard theory (and its extensions) has been a sad disappointment to the AI community, *despite* the fact that it is eminently computational (in Marr's sense). But this is precisely a function of the point I am making. It was assumed that an implementation of it could provide a basis for automated language understanding. But it could not - for that was never the purpose behind its development. Yet Marcus (1980) and others have shown that it *can* be implemented, only on its on (descriptive) terms.

The disenchantment with the standard theory for the purpose of language understanding is one of the ancillary factors behind the development of new computational processes for NL analytic purposes, with unification as the most powerful. But HPSG (for example) is no different from the standard theory in terms of the *kind* of information it makes explicit to the computational process, it only makes *more* available at a finer level of detail. And the change in computational process as such does not constitute a change in the *goal* of computation.

3. The cases of structure preservation and tree admissibility

Emonds' (1976) constraint on transformations known as 'structure preservation' played a decisive role in the development of the standard theory, since it helped to bring out in the open the enormous power of transformations. In a different vein, Gazdar et al.'s (1985) idea that rules be interpreted as conditions on legal trees, has a similar effect on phrase structure grammars.

In both cases, however, we are faced with strictly theory-dependent notions which constrain the *amount* of descriptive information made explicit by a set of rules, not the *kind*.

The conclusion I draw from this is that the wrong kind of information is made explicit by standard NL representations, *as far as language understanding is concerned*. And the remedy would seem to be to develop alternative forms of representation which make explicit different *kinds* of information.

Understanding and interpretation

The alternative to descriptively relevant representations as the proper kind of input to the computations involved in NL understanding, as already intimated, is based on the notion of interpretation. In this section of the paper, therefore, I shall:

- show that the goal of computation indeed is interpretive;
- discuss the notion of interpretation and its relation to understanding;
- introduce and discuss the notion of dynamic text comprehension.

The goal of NL computation

One of the most pervasive differences between current approaches and the one I advocate is the fact that the strings of language that I am interested in are instances of language in *use*. Now, this has nothing to do with the competence-performance distinction. In fact, I assume that the input is invariably grammatical and otherwise 'correct'. What it means, rather, is that whenever I write an input sentence I expect some kind of *response* to it. So, if I were to write (1):

(1) a. Every man who owns a donkey beats it.
    b. What does every man who owns a donkey do to it?
    c. Forget what I just said.

- I would expect some change of intentional state to have occurred in the reader (man or machine) for (a,c), and I would expect a reply (eg. *he beats it*, or *I don't know*) for (b). Ususally in linguistics, sentences are just examples, and their authors do not expect any human reader to form the belief that 'every man who owns a donkey beats it' from reading (1a). He *does*, however, expect the reader to be convinced by, to change his opinions because of, to agree or disagree with, etc., almost everything he writes *outside* the examples in his text. This language-in-use requirement constitutes explicit indication that *interpretation* is the ultimate goal of whatever computational processes I might be inclined to introduce.

Interpretation as a cognitive process
But what, in this context, is interpretation? On a formal semantics approach, interpretation presupposes the translation of NL sentences into disambiguated, wellformed formulas of some formal language, and it amounts to the automatic association of syntactically identified expressions of that language with truth values, objects or sets of objects in a model, possible world or situation (depending on theory). This application of the term 'interpretation' to a function from *formal expressions* to models (etc) is both legitimate and precise. But it presupposes a solution to the non-mechanical, non-trivial and meaning-guided problem of translating NL sentences into wellformed formulas. Forming *that* association is a cognitive feat that might, with equal justification and precision, be termed 'interpretation'. This is precisely the point where syntax is transformed into semantics, where form is informed by content. Whether there *is* such a point is apparently the key issue between 'hardcore' cognitivists like Fodor and those only admitting to 'weak' AI like Searle. It is, in fact, the substance of his slogan that 'syntax is not causal'.

How could we make sense of this cognitive version of interpretation in relation to text comprehension? An immediate first step might be

(2) a. $F(T) = I$

- where some (reading) function F takes the text T as input and returns interpretation I. This doesn't tell us anything - except that reading a text may produce an interpretation of it. Obviously, a further specification of F is required, with due recognition of its temporality, linearity, modularity, etc., etc. Likewise, we need to specify the expected format of I, how it is construed, what it can be used for, etc., etc. This is what J. Hobbs sets out to do, but in relation to a slightly expanded formula (Hobbs 1990, 20):

(2) b. $F(K,T) = I$

Here the interpretation procedure F takes knowledge base or belief system K and text T as input and produces interpretation I. I shall comment on just two passages, to indicate why I consider Hobbs' approach fundamentally misconceived.

> We must have a logical notation in which knowledge can be expressed and into which English texts can be translated. (Hobbs 1990, 41)

This is the fallacy of descriptivism in its purest form. It shows that the format of T required by F is in fact not a NL text, but a formal translation of it. So, T is already the result of cognitive interpretation, a process which Hobbs considers sufficiently illuminated and unproblematic, except for a few "second-order refinements" still under investigation (Hobbs 1990, 42). It is explicitly stated (p. 23) that *I* is supposed to be a formal representation of the *content* of the text. But all it can aspire to being is a formal paraphrase of a formal disambiguation of a NL text, according to the understanding of that text by the author of the disambiguation.

> The knowledge of the world and the language that is required to understand texts must be encoded in what may be called a "knowledge base". It will necessarily be huge, and the project of determining what needs to be represented, how to encode and organize it, and whether or to what extent it is consistent is correspondingly huge. (Hobbs 1990, 42).

The best rejoinder to this is the following provocative - but also stimulating and optimistic - formulation. It is quoted here to suggest that the NL understanding community should begin to look around for alternatives:

> The general trend in the computer vision community was to believe that recognition was so difficult that it required every possible kind of information. The results of this point of view duly appeared a few years later in programs like Freuder's (1974)[1] and Tenenbaum and Barrows' (1976)[2]. In the latter program, knowledge about offices - for example, that desks have telephones on them and that telephones are black - was used to help "segment" out a black blob halfway up an image and "recognize" it as a telephone. Freuder's program used a similar approach to "segment" and "recognize" a hammer in a scene. (Marr 1982, 35-6)

The original formulation of the *CODEXUS*-project - from which some of the ideas expressed in this article represent a heretical breakaway - can be summed up in

(2)   c. $F(T, K_L, D) = I_D$

---

[1] A computer vision system for visual recognition using active knowledge. MIT A.I. Lab Techn. Rep. 345

[2] Experiments in interpretation-guided segmentation. Stanford Research Institute Tech. Note 123.

– where the interpretive procedure F takes text T, the linguistic knowledge base K_L and the evidential demand D as input, returning the interpretation I_D relative to D.

An 'evidential demand' is a 'query' to the text. The original idea behind this notion was the supposition that an interpretation is always partial - and always in response to an explicit or implicit question to the text. No one ever acquires a 'final' interpretation of any text. If they did, literary and other textual criticism would be dead and buried as academic disciplines a long time ago. The range of evidential demands is infinite, from satisfiable queries like *what is the second word on p. 2* to *give me a brief summary of the first five paragraphs* to *why didn't the Swedes attack the English?*[3] to totally irrelevant (and therefore unsatisfiable) ones like *who was the leading male actor in Bullitt?* They were called *evidential* demands, because they were demands for *evidence* that the text had been understood in a way that could serve as the basis for a reply to the query. After all, the only evidence we have that what we say has been understood, is appropriate action on behalf of the listener.

Evidence for text comprehension as a dynamic process
The idea behind the notion of evidential demand, as introduced above, turns out to be much more general and important than at first suspected. Reading a text can be regarded as a process in which the *current* sentence (ie the sentence currently being read) serves as an 'evidential demand' relative to the portion of the text already processed. This is an intuitive way of stating the fact more formally expressed by saying that processing S_i of Text T is a matter of providing an interpretation of S_i relative to the background provided by the interpretation of sentences $S_1..S_{i-1}$ of T. Consider (3, and cf. Fauconnier (1985, 14)):

(3) a. * The girl with green eyes has brown eyes
   b. The girl with green eyes has brown eyes in the picture
   c. Do you remember John's exhibition? The girl with green eyes has brown eyes. I just met her with John.

The sentence *the girl with green eyes has brown eyes* in (a) is perfectly grammatical and interpretable in the cognitive sense, but not, I take it, in the model theoretic sense, for it expresses a contradiction, given the world as we know it. Expanded by a phrase like *in the picture* (b), it is no longer contradictory, so it can be interpreted in both senses. It is then noteworthy that it is perfectly interpretable in both senses in (c), *without* such expansion. Instead it forms part of a text which provides information to facilitate its inter-

---

[3] The test text was about the Battle of Copenhagen.

pretation. I consider cases like (3c) evidence for the essentially *dynamic* nature of NL understanding in general, and text comprehension in particular.

But cases like (3c) provide other types of evidence as well. First of all, they suggest that the context against which a given sentence is interpreted must be some structure held in memory, and hence must be some form of mental representation. Fauconnier (1985) calls them 'mental spaces', Johnson-Laird (1983) 'mental models'. I shall just call them computable representations (CR). Secondly, they suggest that a listener's assignment of truth values to the sentences he hears, and his decision whether a given sentence is a tautology or a contradiction, etc., are decisions made with reference to CRs. Thirdly, and following from the second point, they suggest that the relationship between language and world is mediated by CRs. Lastly, they provide evidence of the need for *information explicitation*.[4] Consider next a text like:

(4) a. Statsministeren *huskede ikke middagsselskabet*, der iflg. Ninn-Hansens forklaring var blevet holdt aftenen før "gulvtæppetalen" i hans private bolig i Charlottenlund. *Denne lapsus* rokker alvorligt ved Statsministerens/*hans troværdighed.
(The Prime Minister *did not recall the dinner party*, which according to Ninn-Hansen's explanation had been held on the eve of "the carpet speech" in his home in Charlottenlund. *This lapse* jeopardizes the PM's/*his credibility.)

b. Statsministeren *huskede ikke middagsselskabet*, der iflg. Ninn-Hansens forklaring var blevet holdt aftenen før "gulvtæppetalen" i hans private bolig i Charlottenlund. *Den lapsus* rokker alvorligt ved Statsministerens/hans troværdighed.
(The Prime Minister *did not recall the dinner party*, which according to Ninn-Hansen's explanation had been held on the eve of "the carpet speech" in his home in Charlottenlund. *That lapse* jeopardizes the PM's/his credibility.)

The evidence provided by examples such as these concerns the *handling* of CRs. First, both (a) and (b) require the simultaneous occurrence of two CRs, one representing the PM's recall of a situation in which no such entity as 'a dinner party' exists, one representing the account by Ninn-Hansen, in which

---

[4] Notice that even (3a) is interpretable in both senses if speaker and listener are watching a painting of a girl at the time of utterance, and the speaker (at least) already knows the girl depicted. In that case, (a) = (c), which also appears from the fact that in neither of these is it made explicit whether the biological girl has green eyes and the painted girl brown, or *vice versa*. In (b), on the other hand, the biological girl has green eyes, the painted one brown.

it does. I take this as evidence that CRs are established *concurrently* and *dynamically*, on the basis of information provided by textual input.

Secondly, the evidence provided by the distribution of *his* as an anaphor to *the Prime Minister* in the context of *this* and *that*, respectively, suggests a distinction between *current* and *accessible*[5] CR. In (a), *this* informs the listener to stay in the current CR, thus interpreting *lapse* as characterizing (the representation of) Ninn-Hansen, whereas, in (b), *that* informs the listener to shift into another, but accessible, CR in which *lapse* characterizes the (representation of the) PM. This distinction is neutralized by *the PM's* instead of *his*. One of the functions of definite descriptions is to inform the listener to look for *some* accessible CR in which an entity will meet the description provided by the lexical material of the description.

Thirdly, (4) provides ample evidence that extreme care should be taken not to confuse the notion of (cognitive) interpretation with the notion of fit. The result of interpretation is the creation of an intentional state with direction of fit towards the world. But whether it *fits* (is 'true') is not just a matter of what the real world is like. It is also a matter of its compatibility with the reader's current CR of the real world. There is no reader independent procedure by which a truth value can be assigned to the last sentence of the text. All that can be said is that it is *presented* as true. Nor does the text carry explicit information that there in fact was a dinner party on the eve of the "carpet speech". It carries explicit information that its author *believes* (and that Ninn-Hansen *claims*) that there was such a party - and (a) only carries this information of author's belief if *his* is not used in the last sentence.

Fourthly, readers with absolutely no 'real world' knowledge of current Danish political scandals are eminently capable of *understanding* (4) - if they read English (or Danish). What they will not be able to do after reading it is answer questions like *who is Ninn-Hansen?, what is the name of the Prime Minister?, what does "gulvtæppetalen" refer to?*, and a host of others. But they *will* be able to answer questions like *where does Ninn-Hansen live?, why is the PM's credibility at risk?*, etc.

The formula for dynamic text comprehension
The evidence presented above leads to the view that text understanding is a process by which CRs are created and manipulated by the reader on the basis of information made explicit by the text. It thus provides a basis for a distinction between 'understanding' and '(cognitive) interpretation', compatible with, if not identical to, the distinction between understanding as a 'second-order capacity' and interpretation as a 'first-order capacity to act' in Chomsky (1975, 22f). Understanding is a complex, higher-order process, consisting of a sequence of lower-order interpretations. Each interpretation is a computation

---

[5] See further below for discussion of the notion of accessibility.

with a specific task and with local effect. Whether understanding can be exhaustively characterized in terms of (computable) interpretations is debatable, but - so far at least - not proven one way or the other. The rest of the paper discusses various consequences of the view that it *can*, which gives rise to the formula (2)(d) as a replacement of (2)(c):

(2) d. $F(T) = < I_1('''',\{CR_0,K_L\},E_1),$
$I_2(E_1,\{CR_0 \supset CR_1,K_L\},E_2),$
....
$I_n(E_{1..n-1},\{CR_0 \supset CR_1 \supset,...,\supset CR_{n-1},K_L\},E_n >$

The process of understanding text T, $F(T)$, is an ordered sequence of local interpretations, I_i. Each I_i is guided by information made explicit by linguistic element E_i. Input is previous linguistic elements $E_{1..i-1}$, a knowledge base, which can be construed as the union of set $\{CR_0, CR_1,..., CR_{i-1}\}$ of computable representations and linguistic knowledge base $\{K_L\}$, plus the current linguistic element, E_i. Linguistic elements may be anything from sentence to phrase to lexical item to morpheme, depending on the nature of I_i. CR_i is the "parent" of CR_{i+1} (cf. Fauconnier 1985, 17). Output is a knowledge base, revised in the light of the interpretation of E_i.

Information and meaning

From what I have argued so far it follows that texts are (also) computable representations. Obviously, and given the basic assumption of the approach taken here, if *writing* a text is a complex process requiring cognitive faculties, then there would be nothing illuminating about such a characterization, since the text would be the final output from the process. On the other hand, using this characterization does highlight one aspect of texts which is relevant to the question of text *comprehension:* a text, *qua* computable representation, must contain the *information* necessary for its own interpretation. Apart from insistence on this point I shall not press the issue, and I should be quite happy to regard texts, *qua* concrete manifestations of NL, as something that contains *meaning*, reserving the term 'computable representation' for whatever internal and intermediate representations are created by interpretive computations.

It might seem pedantic to raise this point, were it not for the fact that it brings out for discussion the relationship between information and meaning. Recall that the CRs produced by interpretive computation are supposed to be, *not* representations of the *meaning* of the text, but (representations of) intentional, mental states with inclination of fit *away* from the text. So the claim is that the information needed by the interpretive processes is made explicit by the meaning of the text.

Situation semantics
The currently most ambitious attempt to provide an information based semantic theory is probably Devlin (1991), which aims to develop a mathematical theory of information flow. The formal constructs (socalled *infons*) of the theory are semantic objects, capturing information about states of affairs in the world in digitalized form. The kind of information that infons capture is the kind the TV News deals in. Infons are descriptive. They are representations of the internal structure of situations. Although he does discuss cognitive issues (pp. 99ff; Ch. 6), it turns out that whatever mental representations ('states' or 'situations') are recognized, they are replicas of representations of external situations. He says nothing about the crucial issue, which is, in his terms, the nature of the *constraint* between an external situation and its internal representation, except that it is what makes the internal representation meaningful with respect to the environment (p.101). It is the basic contention of this paper that this link is computational and interpretive. We need, as it were, to regard information, not as something to be represented, but as something which guides the construction of representations. We need to look for information as *instructions*.

Instruction semantics

> Relatively simple grammatical structures give instructions for space construction in context. (Fauconnier 1985, 2)

The crucial feature of Fauconnier's theory of *Mental Spaces* is its procedural underpinnings. Transposed into our context and terminology, it is based on the following two principles:

- computable representations are created during reading;
- the information needed for the construction of CRs is made explicit by the text itself.

Looking at NL meaning in the light of these points, we are led to the formulation of the central thesis of *Instruction Semantics*:

> *NL meaning is the pervasive phenomenon which provides the information necessary for the interpretive computations of CRs.*

The types of information we are interested in is not the TV news kind, but rather information conveyed by the structural properties of language. It is the possession by NLs of this kind of information which makes the business of creating CRs from NL input a radically different enterprise from creating CRs from non-symbolic input. I call it *interpretive* information.

Types of interpretive information

Interpretive information provided by natural language is of various kinds: syntactic, lexical, inferential, referential and rhetorical. Here I shall confine myself to those structural properties of NP that make referential information explicit. (Cf. Thrane 1992 for a general discussion of some other types of interpretive instructions).

Referential information is needed for the interpretive processes of:

- *classification* of entities;
- *assignment of properties (to entities)*;
- *identification* of entities;
- *individuation* of entities;
- *enumeration* of entities;
- *comparison* of entities.

The structural properties of NP are not in doubt. They are:

- NPs contain N
- NPs may contain A
- NPs contain specifying and complementizing elements other than A
- NPs are recursive
- NPs may be syntactically replaced by variables (PRO)
- NPs may be syntactically replaced by proper names

Where opinions differ, as indicated at great length, is how these facts should be *represented* in linguistic theory. And this question, as also indicated, should be decided with respect to computational *goal*.

Explicitation of referential information

The global understanding of a text is the result of a series of local interpretations. I want to make this claim a bit more specific, by tying it to the discussion of how interpretive information is made explicit and how such information is used. The pertinent tools are those of *level of interpretation* and *accessibility*.

Levels of interpretation and accessibility: classification and identification

The interpretive processes of classification and property assignment are traditionally linked with the fact that NPs contain nouns and adjectives. But the information that a string S is a noun or an adjective isn't very helpful in itself. What would be helpful would be information about the *consequences* of interpreting S as a noun, which are these: if you interpret a string, say *farmer, donkey, water*, as a N, then you accept - and establish, if it isn't already - a category, *cat(FARMER)*, *cat(DONKEY)*, *cat(WATER)*, and regard it as the name of a list of *indices*[6], empty so far. A similar procedure leads to *prop(PRETTY,{})* for adjectives (and - for present purposes - intransitive verbs; cf. below).

(5) a. *cat(FARMER,{})*
    b. *cat(DONKEY,{})*
    c. *cat(WATER,{})*

Nouns may be derivatives or compounds, like *owner, donkeyowner*. So apparently we may establish complex categories like those in (6), where *rel* is the functor for the corresponding interpretation of V_{trans}:

(6) a. *cat(rel(OWN,{<cat(X,Y),cat(Z,W)>})*
    b. *cat(rel(OWN,{<cat(X,Y),cat(DONKEY,Z)>})*

Generally, derivation, compounding and nominalization are grammatical phenomena that trigger processes of lexical decomposition. It could be argued, then, that there is no *cat(FARMER,{})*, but only such structures as

(5) a'. *cat(rel(FARM,{<cat(X,Y),cat(FARM,Z)>}))*
    a". *cat(rel(OWN,{<cat(X,Y),cat(FARM,Z)>}))*

The decision on such matters is the concern of the components of lexical interpretation. What is important here is that they highlight a distinction between different *levels of interpretation*. Using a string N as a noun is an

---

[6] Without going into an ontological debate I suggest that indices be regarded as variables that can take integers (including 0) and ∞ (indefinite or unspecified) as values. When they are not bound, they are represented by variable letters x,y,z,... I propose in this way to solve in a practical way some theoretical problems of CR construction/consultation by quantifiers. The following queries will be true on the minimal conditions specified:

> 'farmer' is a noun? :- cat(FARMER,{});
> are there any farmers? :- cat(FARMER,{∞});
> is there a farmer? :- cat(FARMER,{x}), x<>0;
> there are no farmers? :- cat(FARMER,{0});
> there are three farmers? :- cat(FARMER,{12,x,y}).

I use X,Y,Z... in the notation cat(FARMER,X) to indicate a list of any internal composition. In some respects, indices can be compared to Hans Kamp's [1982] discourse referents.

indication that some category is to be accepted as *cat(N,{})*, irrespectively of what *internal* interpretive (or constructive) processes have led to N. On such a view, (5a) is a lexicalization of (5a') or (5a") or ... Such structures are immediately *accessible* for the purpose of deciding the semantics of *farmer* and other language related discourse. But it is structures like (5a) that will be immediately accessible at levels above that of lexical interpretation. One of these is the level of interpretation of pronouns, which is a matter of identification. Hence (7a,b) cannot have the coreference patterns indicated; *cat(DONKEY,X)* is inaccessible at this level, which only supports *cat(-DONKEYOWNER,X)* and *prop(DONKEYOWNING,X)* as the result of lexicalization of (6b):

(7) a. * every donkey$_i$owner beats it$_i$ /them$_i$
    b. * every donkey$_i$owning farmer beats them$_i$ /it$_i$

Accessibility is a fluid notion, however. It is connected with the notion of explicitation of information, and with the notion of *logical depth*, as the measure of the amount of computation required to reach a result. Consider in this connection data like

(8) a. He saw the car$_i$. It$_i$ was a Dodge Ram.
    b. He saw the car$_i$ crash. It$_i$ was a Dodge Ram.
    c. He survived the car$_i$ crash. It$_i$ was a Dodge Ram.

On the view set out above, the interpretation of *it* in (a) is straightforward: the process has immediate access to *cat(CAR,{17})* - where 17 is index no. 17, already established - and yields a coreferential reading. In (b), interpreting *it* the same way will support a reading of the first sentence on which *crash* is a V, thus possibly providing structure to an otherwise unstructured CR. In (c), however, *cat(CAR,X)* is not immediately accessible for coreference; and yet it could very well be used as a creative piece of advertising. It would be creative because it requires some computation to reach the desired result *Rams are safe cars*. Such examples suggest that the interpretation of pronouns is the result of a search through, and possibly leads to revision of, a number of CRs, some of which are more accessible than others.

Categorial CRs like *cat(DONKEY,X)* have two components, a label and a list of indices. This claim is borne out by data like (7c-d) and (9), which reveal issues of identification.

(7) c. every farmer who owns a donkey$_i$ /donkeys$_j$ beats it$_i$ /them$_j$
    d. every owner of a donkey$_i$ /donkeys$_j$ beats it$_i$ /them$_j$
    e. * every farmer, who owns a donkey$_i$ /donkeys$_j$, beats it$_i$ /them$_j$

(9) The man behind the glove$_i$ is Milan's manager. There are quite a few of those$_i$ around today, for it is bitterly cold.

Interpreting *it* and *them* as coreferential with *donkey* and *donkeys* respectively in (7c) and (7d) is a matter of having access to the indices on the *list* in *cat(DONKEY,X)*. Why is that list accessible in (7c,d), but not in (e)? Because immediate access to *cat(DONKEY,X)* is a precondition on *identifying* the members of the lists in *cat(FARMER,X)* in (7c) and *cat(OWNER,X)* in (7d) of which it is predicated that they beat something. In contrast, the nonrestrictive relative clause in (7e) requires no such access for identification. In that case, identification is assumed by the speaker to be possible on the basis of *cat(FARMER,X)* alone. The nonrestrictive relative clause invites the listener to establish and accept a CR in which every member of his list in *cat(FARMER,X)* is catalogued as the owner of an unspecified number of donkeys, in addition to what other information about them is available. But this is incidental to the interpretation of the pronouns, so the resultant CR is inaccessible to that process.

In (9), the crucial point for pronoun interpretation is not the list, but the label, in *cat(GLOVE,X)*. The second sentence invites the listener to accept that an unspecified number of entities can be identified as, and therefore should be assigned to ∞ in the list labelled, *GLOVE*. It goes on to offer an argument why this should be accepted.

So, categories are CRs of form *cat(X,Y)*, corresponding to the classes denoted by nouns. Nouns *establish categorial locations* for entities. Entities are represented by indices. In the same vein, adjectives (and - for present purposes - intransitive verbs) establish 'property' locations for independently specified entities of the form *prop(X,Y)*. How indices are established, introduced, identified, and otherwise manipulated is the concern of the *referential functives*.

Referential functives: finite state machines?
One of the key linguistic features in this approach is the prominence of the so-called 'grammatical words' (articles, pronouns, auxiliaries, prepositions, etc.). These are the material backbone of language *structure*. Without exhaustive knowledge of them in a given language, we cannot be said to know that language. In contrast, most of us know only a proportion of the lexical items of any of the languages we profess to know. To emphasise this importance I have invented a term for them: *functives*, which is intended to convey their crucial functional properties. The subclass of functives pertinent to NP are the

referential functives. They comprise determiners, pronouns, quantifiers and other closed class elements of NP structure, except prepositions. Cf. Thrane (1979; 1980) for detailed discussion.

Van Benthem (1987) suggests the possibility of implementing quantifiers as various kinds of automata, eg. the universal and existential quantifiers as finite state automata (Fig. 1).

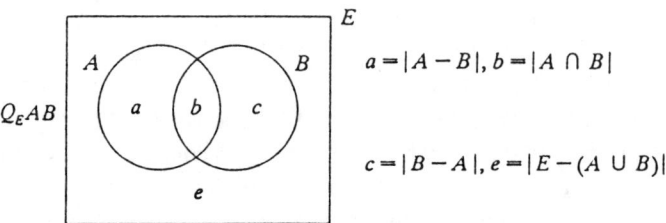

Figure 1: A finite state automaton for the universal quantifier.

This appeal to local interpretive processes is highly attractive. The implicit appeal to a preexisting model is not, at least not on its own. For we need the added possibility of *creating* a model from quantifier interpretation. Consider (10):

(10)   all birds fly

What do you *do* when you hear a sentence like (10)? You are likely to take it as expressing a claim by the speaker about birds in general - that is: wherever in the (real) world there is or has been something you might be willing to classify as a bird, the claim is that it flies sometimes, or that it has the ability to fly if it wanted to. So, it is also a claim about the (real) world. Now, this information is made explicit by the *occurrence* of *all*, plural and the present tense on the verb, and by the *non-occurrence* of the definite article, modal verbs or any other indication of non-factuality.

Suppose you disagree with the claim. What basis do you have for disagreement? Knowledge of just *one* bird somewhere in the real world which *never* flies, or which *can't fly*. Does that commit you to claiming access to *all* birds in the whole world? Obviously not. Access to just one is enough. On the other hand, knowledge of some fictitious bird which never flies does not constitute grounds for disagreement, I don't think, but the point is debatable.

How should this be handled in computational terms? By constructing a representation on the basis of information made explicit by the input sentence, to the effect that:

- there is a category *cat(BIRD,{})* and a property *prop(FLY,{})*, available for the localization of indices (the effect of *birds* and *fly*);
- there are no spatial or temporal constraints on the area in the (real) world which you might care to search for entities to be indexed (the effect of indefiniteness + present tense + factuality);
- there are no constraints on the number of entities that you are allowed to inspect (the effect of *all* + plural);
- for every entity you are prepared to index in *cat(BIRD,{})*, that same index is properly assigned to the list in *prop(FLY,{})* (the effect of the syntactic pattern NP-$V_{intrans}$).

What matters here is the constructive role played by indefiniteness and *all* + plural: the former makes explicit the spatial bounds within which a search for entities is allowed, in this case the entire (real) world, and the latter does not constrain the number of entities over which a search may be made. But it cannot be a question of having access to the whole world in any physical sense. It must be a question of having access to our knowledge of the world. That knowledge is contained in CR_0, so what the combination of *all*, plural and indefinite article does is *guide and constrain our search in CR_{i-1} if we want to*. For there is nothing to keep us from replying 'If you say so', or 'Are you sure'? Nor from creating from the sentence a *rule*, that is, a CR of the form *rule(cat(BIRD,X):-prop(FLY,X))* that may be activated at some later stage.

A hierachy of referential processes?

Devlin (1991, 20f;25) considers our ability to *discriminate* conceptually basic, underlying a more 'conscious' process of individuation. Expanding on this I offer the following tentative and somewhat speculative 'hierarchy' of interpretive processes of referential information:

- individuation is a function of discrimination;
- classification is a function af individuation and categorization;
- property assignment is a function of individuation and localization;
- enumeration is a function of recursive individuation;
- comparison is a function of recursive property assignment;
- identification is a function of recursive classification or property assignment.

The abilities to *categorize* (the realization that two individuals are 'the same' in some respect) and *localize* (the realization that individuals are susceptible to change) are equally 'basic', views that concur at least with such otherwise disparate positions as Lakoff's (1983) and the 'localist' tradition in European linguistics, notably Anderson (1971; 1973; etc.). Apart from this I am quite aware that such attempts at 'reductionism' can easily be rebuffed (cf. Putnam 1973; 1988). Even so, all avenues towards new insight into the workings of NL based on such notions have not yet been travelled. I hope to have pointed to at least an inviting, if so far sparsely traficked, path.

References
Anderson, John M. (1971) *The Grammar of Case*. Cambridge.
Anderson, John M. (1973) 'Maximi Planudis in Memoriam', in: Kiefer, F & N. Ruwet (eds): *Generative Grammar in Europe*. Dordrecht, 20-47.
Chomsky (1975) *Reflections on Language*. London.
Devlin, Keith (1991) *Logic and information*. Cambridge.
Emonds, Joseph E. (1976) *A Transformational Approach to English Syntax: Root, Structure-preserving, and Local Transformations*. New York.
Fauconnier, Gilles (1985) *Mental Spaces*. Cambr. Mass.
Gazdar, Gerald et al. (1985) *Generalized Phrase Structure Grammar*. Oxford.
Hobbs, Jerry R. (1990) *Literature and Cognition*. CSLI, Stanford.
Jackendoff, Ray (1987) 'On Beyond the Zebra: The relation of linguistic and visual information', in: *Cognition* 26, 89-114.
Johnson-Laird, P.N. (1983) *Mental Models*. CUP.
Kamp, Hans (1982) 'A theory of truth and semantic representation', in: Groenendijk, J.A.G. et al (eds): *Formal Methods in the Study of Language*. Mathematical Centre Tracts, 135. Amsterdam, 277-322.
Lakoff, George (1983) *Women, Fire and Dangerous Things*. New York.
Marcus, Mitchell (1980) *A Theory of Syntactic Recognition for Natural Language*. Cambr. Mass.
Marr, David (1982) *Vision*. Cambr. Mass.
Putnam, Hilary (1973) 'Reductionism and the Nature of Psychology', in: Haugeland, John (ed) *Mind Design*. Cambr. Mass. 1985, 207-19.
Putnam, Hilary (1988) *Representation and Reality*. Cambr. Mass. 1989.
Thrane, Torben (1979) 'Concerning the number and nature of word classes', in: Chesnutt, M. et al. (eds): *Publications of the Department of English*, University of Copenhagen, 8, 247-63.
Thrane, Torben (1980) *Referential-semantic analysis*. Cambridge.
Thrane, Torben (1992) 'The fallacy of descriptivism', in: Hansen, S.L. & F. Sørensen (eds): *Issues in Semantic Representation*. Copenhagen.